THE RISE AND FALL OF
HARLAND
AND WOLFF

THE RISE AND FALL OF
HARLAND
AND WOLFF

TOM McCLUSKIE MBE

Dedication

Dedicated to the many thousands who toiled to make
Harland and Wolff great.
*'From this day until the ending of the world
we in it shall be remembered. We few, we band of brothers.'*
Henry V

Acknowledgements

To Sylvia for her unending patience; John and Paddy for their
friendship and encouragement; Valerie for the childhood memories;
Ed and Karen for their support; and finally Abbie, Chrissy and Amy
at The History Press for their faith and trust in the project.

Cover illustrations. Front: Thompson Wharf outfitting quay, with
Thompson dry dock to the right. *Back*: Hard at work building the
best. (Both images author's collection)

First published 2013

The History Press
The Mill, Brimscombe Port
97 St George's Place,
Cheltenham, Gloucestershire, GL50 3QB
www.thehistorypress.co.uk

Reprinted 2017, 2021

British Library Cataloguing in Publication Data.
A catalogue record for this book is available from the British Library.

ISBN 978 0 7524 8861 5

Typesetting and origination by The History Press
Printed by TJ Books Limited, Padstow, Cornwall

Contents

Foreword

On 21 September 1858 Edward Harland received a letter from his employer, Robert Hickson, which was to signal the beginning of a dream. The letter contained an offer from Hickson to sell his shipyard – lock, stock and barrel – to Harland for the princely sum of £5,000, on the condition that he would complete the construction of the *Oceola*, a vessel Hickson was building for himself. Harland eagerly accepted this offer, seeing in it the opportunity to fulfil a long-cherished ambition to own his own shipyard. So it was, on 1 November 1858, that the long-established company of Robert Hickson & Company converted to Edward James Harland & Company. From this inauspicious beginning the foundation stone was laid for a shipbuilding dynasty which would develop into Harland and Wolff, a name recognised throughout the globe as the 'shipbuilder to the world'.

For over 135 years the company continued to prosper and keep alive the spirit and dream of its founder, despite ever-increasing threats to its very existence which emanated from several quarters beginning with the great industrial depression of the 1930s. In common with any large industrial enterprise, Harland and Wolff found itself having to weather many storms, ranging from the loss of perhaps its most famous vessel – RMS *Titanic* – to the severe damage inflicted on its operations by enemy bombing raids during the Second World War. Despite these and several other pitfalls along the way, the future of the company always appeared to be, if not secure, then at least a cornerstone of Northern Ireland's economy, and as such would survive regardless of any economic difficulties it encountered. Alas, like with *Titanic*, an unexpected disaster was looming on the horizon which would see the company founder and destroy Edward Harland's dream forever.

Introduction

RMS *Titanic* & the Beginning

Harland and Wolff Ltd remains to this day the most universally recognised name in shipbuilding. Located in Belfast, Northern Ireland, the company was established during the critical developmental years of one of the most important transportation technologies to emerge from the Industrial Revolution: the steam-powered ocean-going ship. Edward Harland and Gustav Wolff entered into partnership in 1861 as two talented and forward-thinking shipbuilders. Together, their radical departure from the accepted designs and engineering methods for constructing ocean-going steamships would become the standard by which all other ships were measured. Indeed, Harland and Wolff can be credited with the design of the first, true, modern ocean liner – the White Star passenger ship *Oceanic* – a basic design which is still recognisable in the hull form of passenger ships today.

Steadily, throughout the second half of the nineteenth century, the shipyards of Harland and Wolff became renowned across the world for the excellence of their products. By the turn of the century, the huge complex on Queen's Island on the River Lagan was building the finest ships in the world. Their craftsmanship would become legendary, yet ironically the company today is most closely associated with the creation of just one ship (at its completion it represented one of the greatest technological achievements of the era, and the greatest disaster in commercial steamship history), RMS *Titanic*. Designed to cross the perilous North Atlantic in safety and luxury hundreds of times throughout its service life, alas the unfortunate destiny of *Titanic* was to see her lying at the bottom of the ocean only four days into her maiden voyage in 1912.

Although a dreadful blow to the reputation of Harland and Wolff, the company forged ahead in continuing to produce many remarkable vessels throughout the twentieth century, and in doing so contributed significantly to the war effort during both world wars. With the dramatic changes brought by the introduction of the jetliner in the early 1960s, Harland and Wolff adapted to the evolving marketplace by focusing their efforts on bulk carriers for grain, ore or coal

Right: Edward J. Harland. (All images are
Author's Collection)

Below: The four initial partners at a board meeting, from
left to right: Gustav Wolff, Walter Wilson, William Pirrie
and Edward Harland.

cargoes, plus specialised oil tankers, to meet the growing demand for purpose-designed and -built marketable vessels.

Nevertheless, the shipping industry continued to change with alarming speed and new global market dynamics brought challenging international competition, primarily with cheaper labour costs and new shipbuilding technologies. To further complicate this state of affairs, politically motivated policy changes and accords between Great Britain and the emerging European Economic Community (EEC) dramatically impacted government investment and incentives for British shipyards, all of which was to have a devastating effect on British shipbuilding, and Harland and Wolff in particular.

Despite being acknowledged as the premier shipbuilding enterprise in the world, Harland and Wolff gradually began to lose this dominance. Ironically, as the company struggled with the changing realities of its existing industry, the dark shadow of its past began to re-emerge in the late 1950s as *Titanic* once again became the focus of renewed interest; an interest that would continue to build with increasing momentum throughout the remainder of the century and into the next.

One man (perhaps unwittingly) began to revive the world's interest in a ship the company management would much sooner have seen left forever in the past. A new generation of both amateur and professional historians emerged throughout the remainder of the twentieth century and, not only did the tragic story of RMS *Titanic* make an unwelcome return, the ship itself seemingly materialised from its watery oblivion in a massive blaze of international media attention. Ironically, as Harland and Wolff began its slow and remorseless collapse, its fame rose in contrary proportion, beginning with a single book published in 1955.

In was in that year that an unknown New York City copywriter named Walter Lord came to prominence with the publication of his first book *A Night to Remember*. As a boy, Lord, in company with his parents, had travelled the North Atlantic on the ageing but still grand White Star liner RMS *Olympic*. It was there, aboard *Titanic's* almost identical sister ship, that the young Walter Lord developed what would become a lifetime fascination with the story of *Titanic's* tragic maiden voyage. While the epic tale of *Titanic's* one and only fateful voyage had captivated and stunned the world in 1912, her story had slowly faded into insignificance in the wake of the two world wars which followed her sinking. Lord, however, never lost his childhood obsession with this unique maritime tragedy, spending much of his personal time researching the event and corresponding and speaking with many of *Titanic's* still-living survivors. *A Night to Remember* represented the culmination of Lord's years of labour, and resulted in arguably the most comprehensive account ever written of the tragedy. His book not only became a bestseller in 1955, but continues to be regularly reprinted today over half a century later.

In the wake of Lord's success, many groups and organisations sprang up across the globe, each one dedicated to studying every aspect of the ship and her tragic loss, while inadvertently making Walter Lord the unchallenged authority on the subject until his death in 2003. In 1959 a film based upon the book riveted audiences with the haunting, almost surreal story of the world's newest, largest and most magnificent liner as she slowly foundered on her first voyage across the Atlantic, leaving some 1,500 passengers and crew to face an icy death for lack of lifeboats.

Forty-seven years after her demise, *Titanic* once again sailed into the world's spotlight, producing not only a new generation of enthusiastic amateur *Titanic* historians, but an explosion of myths and legends about the ship and the companies which built and owned her. Among the hundreds of thousands of Lord's readers, one man would go on to contribute a final, dramatic piece to the *Titanic* puzzle. A marine geologist with an abiding interest in the deepest recesses of the world's oceans, Dr Robert Ballard was to find himself adding a new and exciting chapter to the story of RMS *Titanic*.

A tenured professor of the world-famous Woods Hole Oceanographic Institution, located on the shores of Massachusetts in America, Ballard had already made a name for himself in 1977 with the discovery of giant hot air vents located some 9,000ft below the Pacific Ocean near the Galapagos Islands. Crucial to his continuing studies of the ocean's depths was the development of new types of submersible technology equipped to withstand the crushing pressures while exploring the extreme depths of the ocean. The result, achieved through considerable financial support from the United States Navy, had been the creation of a remote-controlled, deep-sea submersible packed with lighting, video and photographic equipment to record the wonders of an alien world far beneath the surface of the world's oceans. Like so many others, Ballard had, from childhood, been fascinated by Walter Lord's definitive book on the *Titanic* disaster. Not surprisingly, the decision was made to test Woods Hole's latest submersible technology by attempting to find the long-lost wreck of *Titanic*, known to be lying at a depth of at least 2 miles on the ocean floor. Though officially labelled as a secondary purpose of the original and classified mission, finally locating *Titanic* would be the ultimate achievement in marine exploration.

As events would unfold, Dr Ballard's research team, which included the French National Institute of Oceanography (IFREMER), became the first to glimpse the massive hull of *Titanic* since the early morning of 15 April 1912, when she finally slipped beneath the waves. Some thirty years after the release of *A Night to Remember*, ghostly images of the legendary liner flickered on to the television monitors aboard the research vessel *Knorr*.

Regrettably, with time and finances rapidly becoming exhausted, Dr Ballard's remote cameras were only able to capture brief, tantalising and frustratingly incomplete images of the long-lost wreck. Nevertheless, news of the discovery made headline news across the world and the intensity of media attention surprised Dr Ballard.

Returning the following summer with a manned submersible, Dr Ballard slowly began a comprehensive analysis of the wreck site. With the aid of side scan radar, it was soon ascertained that the area of the wreckage site covered a vast expanse of the seabed. Until the discovery of the wreck, most experts had settled on the assumption that *Titanic* had sunk to the bottom in one piece, but while the bows and forward section remained majestic and recognisable, it became evident that the huge ship had, in fact, broken up during the sinking. Beyond the severed bow section, a huge debris field stretched for miles across the seabed, eventually leading to the devastated remains of *Titanic*'s stern, located nearly a third of a mile away. The debris field itself was littered with thousands of articles that had spilled from the broken hull on its descent.

Sadly, nearly all of *Titanic*'s magnificent woodwork and her legendary grand staircase were gone, eaten away by the millions of tiny sea creatures which inhabited the wreck.

After the completion of Ballard's second visit to the wreck site, he publicly expressed his desire for the wreck of *Titanic* to be left untouched as a sacred memorial to the 1,523 men, women and children who had perished aboard her that fateful night. Unhappily, such noble and praiseworthy principles were in the main ignored. While legislation was quickly passed in the United States, the United Kingdom and France to prevent the sale of any artefact retrieved from the wreck, a salvage company titling itself RMS Titanic Inc. instituted a legal challenge to these safeguards and eventually succeeded in securing sole salvage rights to the wreck. Unfortunately, Dr Ballard had not pursued claiming salvage rights or ownership of the wreck for either Woods Hole Oceanographic Institution or himself; with hindsight, given the subsequent plundering of the wreck site, this was a decision he came to bitterly regret.

The result of granting salvage rights to RMS Titanic Inc. has been to create two distinct and diametrically opposed expressions of opinion: on the one hand are those agreeing with Dr Ballard that *Titanic* and indeed any other submerged site of historical value should be left pristine and untouched; on the other are those recommending the recovery and preservation of artefacts for future generations to study. To date, the latter section of opinion has prevailed with the result that over the past ten years, RMS Titanic Inc. has visited the wreck site on several occasions and recovered thousands of relics from the debris field. While it is true that the company is legally prevented from selling any of these artefacts, the company continues to generate vast income today from staging exhibitions of the reclaimed items, ostensibly as an attempt to recoup the enormous costs of their salvage missions.

Another resurgence of interest in *Titanic* came with the production of what at the time was the most expensive film ever made in entertainment history. Director James Cameron's film *Titanic* swept the board at the Academy Awards in 1997 with its lavish depiction of her maiden voyage. Cameron meticulously recreated many of *Titanic*'s famous interiors and built a near full-scale model of the ship in what was a car park in Baja, Mexico. Meanwhile, back in the studios in California, the latest digital technologies were used to produce in breathtaking detail the final days of the great liner. The production became the highest ever grossing film in history, recovering its unprecedented $200 million costs several times over.

Like so many before him, Cameron became captivated by the wreck and, in 2001, equipped with specially designed mini-robots and two manned submersibles, he dived to the site on an extraordinary quest to film the interiors of the forward section of *Titanic*'s hull. The resulting documentary revealed what no other expedition had ever seen. Deep within the protection of her hull, the grand dining saloon revealed the still-intact stained-glass windows and richly carved woodwork. The millionaire's suite occupied by Bruce Ismay still bore traces of its once-sumptuous decor; the coal-burning fireplace with its magnificent mantelpiece remained well preserved – last seen by the managing director of the White Star Line as he abandoned his suite some eighty-nine years before. Everywhere, haunting traces of the world's greatest liner resonated back to a time and place when kings ruled mighty empires and the world had yet to experience the devastating consequences of a global war and the massive social upheaval that would ensue. With each wave of renewed interest in *Titanic* and her builders, Harland and Wolff found themselves inundated by requests for information about the ship. It was not a situation in which the company's management found itself entirely at ease.

Despite the history of *Titanic* being so widely known, the story of Harland and Wolff is much more obscure and so in the following chapters I hope to present a much broader and in-depth history of a company which continued to lead the way in the development of innovative design and shipbuilding construction methods, much of which still forms the basis for modern shipbuilding. From the adoption of hydrodynamic hull forms to innovative propulsion systems, Harland and Wolff was a company without equal in pushing the boundaries of shipbuilding technology. Having its roots in Edwardian Belfast, Harland and Wolff did much to create the social framework of the city by providing much-needed work for the mass of the indigenous population, and in doing so also attracted vast numbers of workers to the city. Around the shipyard area huge numbers of terraced houses began to appear to accommodate this influx of workers. This in turn created additional business opportunities for small shopkeepers and, of course, the ubiquitous public houses, where a tired workforce would gratefully slake their thirst built up over a day of strenuous labour, building some of the world's most famous and sometimes some rather notorious ships.

This tight-knit community was almost a village within the city. Streets had familiar names related to Harland and Wolff, such as the obvious Harland Street, Wolff Street and, of course, Island Street, together with perhaps the less obvious but no less pertinent street names of Baltic, Mersey, Lagan or Dock. Almost everyone in this enclave which lay parallel to the Harland and Wolff shipyard along the east side of the River Lagan worked for the company in one capacity or another. A tremendous sense of community was thus established whereby anyone from outside the area was viewed almost with suspicion. Generations of 'Island folk', as they regarded themselves, followed one another into the shipyard and in doing so forged a tradition that has sadly been lost today. The pride these families had in the vessels their menfolk laboured and frequently shed blood over was unique in the history of the City of Belfast. It could rightly be said that Harland and Wolff built the City of Belfast just as much as the ships it constructed on the Queen's Island. Employment for thousands of skilled men and labourers flowed outwards from the vast shipyards of Harland and Wolff; from the rope works to the linen mills, from the steel mills to the textile factories, goods and services were fed into the maw of the shipyard and converted into a completed vessel to sail the world's oceans proudly bearing the legend 'Made by Harland and Wolff, Belfast' on a brass plaque on her bridge front.

Genesis of a Disaster

It had been in late 1907 that Harland and Wolff officially received the commission to build RMS *Titanic* and two sister ships from its oldest and most valued customer, the White Star Line, which had recently become part of a huge American-owned shipping trust: the International Mercantile Marine Company (IMMC). The contract had come in the wake of the introduction of the world's first true superliners, Cunard's *Lusitania* and *Mauretania*. In 1908 these two massive vessels dwarfed any ship ever before built. Nearly 800ft in length and weighing over 30,000 gross tons, the two powerful leviathans could cross the Atlantic at an average running speed of over 25 knots. These new twin Cunarders became an instant success with the wealthy European and American elite, as well as the lucrative immigrant trade. Faced with Cunard's unbeatable twins, IMMC/White Star was obliged to take up the obvious challenge to its position in what had become the never-ending battle for transatlantic steamship supremacy over the past sixty years. Given the task of providing White Star with vessels suitable to carry the fight to Cunard, Harland and Wolff found themselves facing a daunting challenge.

Under the chairmanship of Lord William Pirrie, Harland and Wolff agreed to push the boundaries of marine engineering once again to the limit of what was theoretically achievable. Planned to be over 100ft longer and 10,000 gross tons heavier than the Cunard leviathans, the initial design work on the new ships commenced in March 1908. The first two of the three sister ships would be built side by side in a newly constructed dual slipway at the Queen's Shipyard, alongside the River Lagan. The skills of some of the world's most talented designers and engineers were enlisted for the project, including Alexander Carlisle, the managing director of Harland and Wolff, and Lord Pirrie's accomplished nephew, Thomas Andrews, who was earmarked to succeed Carlisle after his retirement in 1909. Over the next three years the huge new liners, *Olympic* and *Titanic*, slowly grew to dominate Belfast Harbour under a huge metal gantry designed specifically for the purpose. Everything about the two liners was on a colossal scale, including a workforce of some 14,000 men dedicated to the construction of each hull.

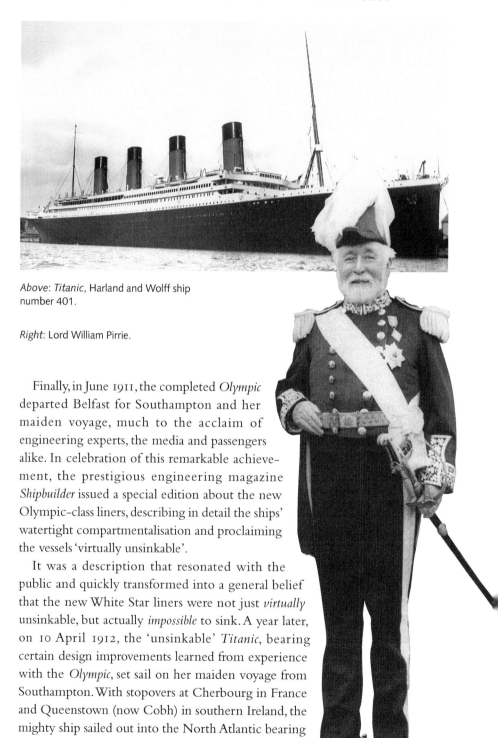

Above: Titanic, Harland and Wolff ship number 401.

Right: Lord William Pirrie.

Finally, in June 1911, the completed *Olympic* departed Belfast for Southampton and her maiden voyage, much to the acclaim of engineering experts, the media and passengers alike. In celebration of this remarkable achievement, the prestigious engineering magazine *Shipbuilder* issued a special edition about the new Olympic-class liners, describing in detail the ships' watertight compartmentalisation and proclaiming the vessels 'virtually unsinkable'.

It was a description that resonated with the public and quickly transformed into a general belief that the new White Star liners were not just *virtually* unsinkable, but actually *impossible* to sink. A year later, on 10 April 1912, the 'unsinkable' *Titanic*, bearing certain design improvements learned from experience with the *Olympic*, set sail on her maiden voyage from Southampton. With stopovers at Cherbourg in France and Queenstown (now Cobh) in southern Ireland, the mighty ship sailed out into the North Atlantic bearing a complement of over 2,200 passengers and crew. She would never return.

Four days after departing Southampton, in the dead of night, *Titanic* touched the side of an iceberg and in less than three hours lay 2 miles beneath the waters of the North Atlantic. By quite a large margin it was, and remains, the worst peacetime maritime disaster in the history of the North Atlantic route. Two major inquiries into the sinking were held in the United States and Great Britain. Both investigations, although conducted in radically different manners, ultimately reached the same conclusions.

RMS *Titanic* had been sailing at an excessive speed for the conditions she was encountering and in spite of several wireless warnings of a massive ice field in her path. Nonetheless, neither inquiry specifically affixed any blame on the White Star Line, the captain or officers in command of the ship. The decision reached was that the tragedy had ultimately been nothing more than a catastrophic series of unfortunate circumstances and no laws of existing navigation or life-saving equipment or procedures had been broken.

Unlike its American counterpart, the British inquiry concentrated on the technicalities of *Titanic*'s construction, navigation and collision damage. It was in this investigation that Harland and Wolff, and especially Lord Pirrie, the company's chairman, experienced some rather uncomfortable moments. Called to give testimony to the inquiry were two key members of Harland and Wolff's senior staff. One was Alexander Carlisle, who although retired from the company before the completion of *Olympic* and *Titanic*, had been the company's managing director and a central figure in the design of both ships.

Carlisle testified to Harland and Wolff having originally specified each vessel to be equipped with a total of forty-eight lifeboats operated under the newly designed Welin Quadrant 'double-acting' davits which were capable of launching multiple lifeboats. Carlisle, who was a brother-in-law to Lord Pirrie, hesitated when asked why this number of lifeboats was not used. While admitting that he had submitted plans to White Star indicating just such a complement of lifeboats, he said that he did not have the power to insist on such an unprecedented number of boats being approved by the vessels' owner.

He further testified that in accepting Harland and Wolff's recommendations for the Olympic-class vessels, White Star could find itself in the uncomfortable and expensive position of retrofitting additional lifeboats to its entire passenger fleet. In the end it was agreed with the White Star Line that the Olympic class should be equipped with the minimum number of lifeboats required by the current Board of Trade regulations. However, as can be imagined, this statement did nothing to enhance the credibility of either the Board of Trade, Harland and Wolff, or its principal customer, the White Star Line.

Also giving testimony was Edward Wilding, a naval architect with Harland and Wolff, who had worked closely with Thomas Andrews on the plans for *Olympic* and *Titanic*. Andrews had been lost in the wreck and so it was left to Wilding to explain the details of *Titanic*'s design and construction. Wilding proved to be an excellent witness, providing the inquiry with a wide range of technical information about *Titanic* and his opinion as to why the 'unsinkable' liner had been anything but. Wilding pointed out that *Titanic*'s fate had been sealed by the lower height of the transverse bulkhead between her fifth and sixth watertight compartments, which only went as high as E deck at the bow. Had this bulkhead been brought up to D deck, it was theoretically possible, said Wilding, that *Titanic* may have survived, or at least remained afloat long enough for rescue vessels to reach her in time. Unfortunately, as he was later to discover, Wilding's candid testimony did anything but endear him to Lord Pirrie.

Certainly his evidence could be construed to suggest that Harland and Wolff had unintentionally built its greatest ships with fatal flaws. The inquiry had also revealed that damage similar to that sustained by *Titanic* would not have caused Cunard's *Lusitania* or *Mauretania* to sink. In the public outcry which followed the *Titanic* disaster, there was almost a witch hunt to attach blame to whomever it would stick. Would-be experts of every sort publicly pontificated on the causes of the tragedy and its possible remedies. For a time, a mild sort of mass public hysteria rained down upon the entire shipping industry and the calls for reform were sometimes extreme and even ludicrous.

The loss of *Titanic* had placed Lord Pirrie and Harland and Wolff in an awkward position, with Pirrie struggling to maintain a firm grip on his company and retain his many clients – most importantly the massive IMMC shipping combine. The largest of American financiers, J.P. Morgan's massive undertakings to dominate and regulate the transatlantic trade, IMMC, had become a monumental failure. Largely influenced by Pirrie in 1902, Morgan's dream of controlling the shipbuilding trade through IMMC was now in jeopardy. Within weeks of *Titanic*'s sinking, her sister ship *Olympic* was back at Harland and Wolff undergoing a massive retrofit, including a partial double hull and heightened watertight bulkheads, along with enough lifeboats for every person aboard.

Britannic, the last of the Olympic-class trio, commenced building in 1912 and incorporated all of the structural changes mandated by the loss of *Titanic*. Slightly larger and longer than her sisters, *Britannic* also featured a vastly different design of launching davits for her greatly increased complement of lifeboats. The davits were novel in design but presented a remarkable eyesore, utterly destroying the sleek beauty of her earlier sisters. *Olympic*'s enormous and costly refit coupled with *Britannic*'s dramatic design improvements were blatant testimony to the safety hysteria predicated by a much less confident travelling public. Harland and Wolff, together with the White Star Line, were obviously determined to restore public confidence in their ships and meekly conceded to almost every demand for change, however pointless it might prove to be.

The talented Edward Wilding, so much a part of the building of *Olympic* and *Titanic*, would not survive his truthful testimony at the British inquiry. Pirrie unceremoniously removed Wilding by enforcing his retirement from the company on medical grounds shortly after his return to Belfast. Pirrie personally, and indeed unfairly, regarded the unfortunate naval architect as the prime cause of *Titanic's* demise, and almost certainly blamed the hapless designer for the untimely death of Pirrie's much-loved nephew, Thomas Andrews. In 1912 such a unilateral and unfair dismissal of a talented marine architect was unremarkable, but it was symptomatic of a trend that remained a typical feature of employment in Harland and Wolff to the very end.

The loss of *Titanic* inevitably reflected badly on Harland and Wolff, and resulted in an unspoken but rigidly enforced policy never to publicly discuss the ship afterwards. Initiated by the intensely private and imperious Lord Pirrie, all files and plans for the ill-fated liner were locked away securely. Decades later, Lord's book of 1955, and the increasing interest in *Titanic* which followed, only hardened Harland and Wolff's unwritten policy of secrecy. Any requests for information or plans of the ship were rebuffed with the simple explanation that all documentation had been destroyed in the bombings of Belfast during the Second World War. In reality, this was a bare-faced lie.

In his final book about *Titanic, The Night Lives On,* the late Walter Lord mused on the seemingly immortal interest in the history of the doomed liner. Even he, the world's most recognised authority on the ship, was at pains to explain the extraordinary phenomenon of *Titanic's* ceaseless fascination as it passed from one generation to the next. Greater and more catastrophic events had filled the twentieth century. Millions had died in war. Systematic genocide and man-made disasters had blighted the world since 1912. Yet *Titanic* remained a cause célèbre in the collective conscience – an everlasting metaphor for modern disaster. 'No story is too farfetched as long as it bears the magic label "Titanic",' wrote Lord. Inevitably, anything and anyone with even the most tenuous association with the ship became the subject of endless discussion, examination, legend and eventually myth, with Harland and Wolff ranking very high on that list.

The spectre of *Titanic* has created a myopic viewpoint of the company which designed and built her. Historians have tended to fuse ship and shipbuilder into a single entity, bestowing the same monumental and legendary attributes on both. Like *Titanic* herself, Harland and Wolff has become fixed in time; a time when the company was one of the largest and most prolific shipbuilding enterprises in the world. In 1998 Michael McCaughan, curator of Maritime History at the Ulster Folk and Transport Museum, described Harland and Wolff in his excellent book *The Birth of Titanic* as 'a shipbuilding company that has always been, and continues to be, at the leading edge of naval architecture and marine technology'. It is an understandable misconception, bolstered by the explosion of books, documentaries and films which have emanated from the epicentre of Ballard's 'titanic' discovery and the absence of any comprehensive historical work about Harland and Wolff.

Employing at its zenith as many as 65,000 men and women, and representing the lifeblood of Belfast for the majority of its existence, the shipyards of Harland

and Wolff today are completely devoid of almost everything associated with its illustrious past. Gone are the vast engine works and massive building sheds and slipways, replaced with ultra-modern office blocks, apartment houses and even a luxury hotel. What had been a virtual wasteland of empty space occupied by only a fraction of its once-enormous workforce, the Queen's Island complex has been reborn from the ashes of Harland and Wolff. Shipbuilding may have ceased there forever, but the ghosts of the past can still be strongly felt today amidst the glass and concrete edifices that dominate the area. The question still remains, however, of why this once mighty and powerful maritime colossus has come to such a piteous and ignoble end. The answer lies in a complexity of reasons, many of which have, until now, remained outside the grasp of maritime historians. It is the objective of this book to examine the history of Harland and Wolff from a unique insider's perspective, and in doing so perhaps some new insights will finally be shed upon what is arguably the most recognised name in world shipbuilding.

For more than thirty years I worked for Harland and Wolff, rising through the ranks of the company to become one of its youngest managers. During those years I took upon myself an unofficial role – one which contradicted the company's age-old policy of rebuffing any public requests for historical information. My newly acquired managerial position, obtained in 1982, placed within my influence the company's massive and chaotic archive of historical

The Harland and Wolff former main office block today.

documents and files. Slowly, and as time allowed, I began a quest to review these important yet all-but-forgotten files.

It became a personal mission to research and preserve as much of the history as I could of what I believed to be Belfast's enormous contribution to British and indeed global maritime engineering. Approaching my immediate superior, the chief technical manager, I sought and received implicit but at the same time informal approval to begin a systematic correlation of the hundreds of thousands of items in the collection into some kind of comprehensible order. The deeper into this vast archive I delved, the more I realised the enormous historical value of the documents. Here was a record of the lifeblood of not simply the company, but of Belfast itself. It was a treasure trove of important maritime history which I became determined to both preserve and make available to current and future generations of maritime historians. I was mindful of the terrible loss which had occurred sometime after 1934 when the merger of the famous White Star Line and Cunard resulted in most of White Star's documents being thrown away.

The Harland and Wolff archive contained the most comprehensive record of RMS *Titanic* from her conception until her tragic loss in April 1912. Far from being hidden away in a secure location, I felt such monumentally important documents should be brought once more into the light and allowed to take their rightful place in the history of this great company. Not only did I see great historical value in the Harland and Wolff archives, but a potentially positive and financially remunerative service which the company could provide to the countless enquiries not only concerning *Titanic*, but many of the other famous ships built by the company.

Initially, my radical view was not shared by the company's public affairs department, but their uneasiness over my initiative was reduced to memos cautioning me against giving away 'family' secrets. However, the success of my programme led to a request to make a full presentation to the Board of Directors. There, I forcefully argued my case, suggesting that co-operation and the sharing of historical documents could only serve to enhance the company's name and prestige, as well as generate a new source of income. In a majority vote the Board agreed, much to the displeasure of the chief executive who, on more than one occasion, sought to obstruct my efforts.

What follows is a personal perspective of the founding of a shipbuilding dynasty until its inevitable and sad decline, as it struggled to cope with a world rapidly changing in both financial and technological demands in the production of vessels. Taken from my own knowledge derived from a career with the company, I hope that my discoveries and singular experience will provide an intimate insight into one of the greatest shipbuilders the world has ever known. As this book is a reflection of my own experiences and opinions, I must therefore take responsibility for any errors or omissions it may contain.

2

The Emergence of the Port of Belfast

The city and port of Belfast, Northern Ireland, has been associated with the building of ships for well over 300 years, with the first vessels being recorded as completed in 1663. Sadly, this fine tradition of craftsmanship and excellence in the field of marine engineering has declined into the shadows of past glories. The slipways and building berths of Harland and Wolff that once saw the construction of such magnificent vessels as RMS *Titanic*, *Canberra* and *Southern Cross* now lie derelict and forlorn, as ghostly and silent witnesses to the demise of a once-mighty industrial complex and a golden age of shipbuilding. In writing this history I will inevitably touch upon some of the more elusive and little-known aspects behind the slow but deliberate decimation of the company. To understand and appreciate the magnitude of these misguided and sometimes reckless acts of corporate policy, I need first to return to a different time and era when ships became the lifeblood of the emerging British Empire; an empire which was destined to become possibly the greatest the world has ever known.

The River Lagan flows through the heart of the City of Belfast and has provided a solid foundation for the steady rise in the prosperity of the city, allowing merchants and traders ready access to ocean-going vessels. The establishment of this burgeoning commercial trade led naturally to the requirement for some sort of repair facility to service and maintain these vessels. Over time this would evolve into actual shipbuilding operations and eventually into the formation of the massive Harland and Wolff complex of shipyards and engineering works. However, before this giant enterprise emerged there would be several false starts, trials and challenges along the way.

Thanks to much environmental effort through various generations of City Fathers, the River Lagan today is a clean and relatively straight waterway far removed from its original course which meandered in a narrow and twisting manner through the city in the eighteenth century. At that time, the ever-increasing use of the river for commerce and trade prompted the establishment of the Belfast Harbour Commissioners in 1785, who took for themselves the grandiose title of The Corporation for Preserving and Improving the Port and Harbour of the City of Belfast. This august body of gentlemen, mainly comprised of merchants and traders, initiated an ambitious, long-term programme of improvements to the quays and wharves along the banks of the river. The dramatic changes began to pay handsome dividends when William Ritchie, an established shipbuilder from the fishing port of Saltcoats on the Ayrshire coast of Scotland, visited Belfast in 1791.

Even at this point in the reconstruction, Ritchie was tremendously impressed with the improved deep-water port facilities, offering as they did the potential for the expansion of Ritchie's long-established shipping business on the mainland. After a warm and enthusiastic reception by the Corporation, Ritchie returned to Scotland and quickly set about drawing up a comprehensive plan for a new shipbuilding yard to be located on the west bank of the River Lagan. Back in Belfast, his impressive plans prompted the Commissioners to add an additional incentive to their prospective investor. They would give Ritchie the exclusive use of a docking platform upon which vessels could be raised out of the water for hull cleaning and repair. The deal was officially confirmed and William Ritchie's new Belfast shipping enterprise became the cornerstone of a tradition of shipbuilding and marine engineering that would last two centuries.

Canberra, Harland and Wolff ship number 1621, the last passenger liner built by the company.

Southern Cross, Harland and Wolff ship number 1498, one of the first passenger liners to have aft placed engines.

Belfast's new port facilities soon attracted the avid attention and investment of other mainland industrialists, prompting the Harbour Commissioners to energetically underwrite even greater improvements to the now burgeoning port. The final phase included a monumental engineering project to straighten, deepen and widen the river. This long-term plan meant creating two massive straight cuts directly towards the mouth of Belfast Lough and the sea beyond. Work on the first straight cut began in 1837 and, upon completion in 1841, was immediately followed by the second and final straight cut. In January 1849 the Port of Belfast could now boast one of the finest port and shipping facilities in Great Britain.

The excavations to straighten the river had resulted in the removal of millions of tons of spoil and debris, which had been transported and dumped at the mouth of the river along the eastern shoreline. This enormous amount of displaced earth grew over the years of construction to form a huge, artificial island which came to be known as Queen's Island in honour of Queen Victoria, who officially opened the magnificent new port facilities in August 1849. As a major shipbuilding and ocean-going port, Belfast had come of age, and with each passing year yielded ever-increasing ocean-bound traffic and shipping business to the city.

The greatest payoff of the initiatives of Belfast's Harbour Commissioners would come with the arrival of a young 23-year-old engineering apprentice, hired to manage the failing shipbuilding yard of an iron manufacturer named Robert Hickson. Edward Harland was truly a man of his time. The Industrial Revolution was in full swing, exploding with new inventions and remarkable advances in science and the growing field of applied engineering. Imagination seemed boundless, and new and daring commercial enterprises shook the world almost to its foundations. It is not an overstatement to say that Harland would become a living legend of his era and one of the most brilliant marine engineers of the nineteenth century.

3

Steaming into the Future

E dward Harland was born in May 1831 in Scarborough, Yorkshire. He was the sixth child of Dr William Harland, a successful and well-respected medical practitioner who had also established something of a reputation as a talented inventor, having designed, built and patented his own version of a steam carriage in 1827. From his earliest years, his son Edward had also displayed a talent for engineering and, by his own admission, frequently neglected his academic studies to observe the local engineers at work, often volunteering to help at any opportunity. His keen interest was not that surprising. Edward's father was a close personal friend and confidant to the scientist and engineer George Stephenson, who had become famous through his development of the first practical steam locomotive. In 1825 Stephenson had built England's first railway between Stockton and Darlington. In 1830 he went on to build the first railway between two major English cities – Liverpool and Manchester – designing not only the locomotives, but rolling stock and rails as well. It is little wonder then, given such illustrious mentors, that Edward Harland saw himself in the heroic image of Stephenson. Modern engineering, the advances in steam propulsion and iron making electrified the young and ambitious Harland. It was an age of unbounded scientific invention, and visionaries such as Edward Harland were captivated with the possibilities.

While Dr William Harland harboured hopes that his son would soon tire of his obsession and return to his studies as a barrister, Edward remained determined to become a professional engineer. In 1846, having completed his grammar school education, he promptly joined the company of George Stephenson's son, Robert Stephenson & Company of Newcastle, where he was hired as an apprentice. During this five-year apprenticeship, Edward became deeply interested in the design of ships and the practicalities of shipbuilding. A particular preoccupation he developed at this time concerned the enormous loss of life among seafarers. Accordingly, Harland began experimenting with a revolutionary design for a new type of lifeboat which featured a hand-powered propeller at each end. Unveiling his prototype in 1850, the young Harland learned an important lesson. Ship owners were a highly conservative group, more interested in profits than radical new technologies. His new lifeboat was viewed with suspicion and rejected as both unnecessary and costly.

Nevertheless, as time and history would prove, Edward Harland was not a man to be easily thwarted. In the blossoming field of engineering, Harland was a true modern, and he continued to develop his ideas and concepts for improving the technology of seagoing vessels. It was at this point in his early career that fate played a pivotal role in Harland's life. Immersed in his apprenticeship, he met and was befriended by an associate of Edward's father.

An expatriate of Hamburg, where he had been born in 1815, Gustav Christian Schwabe was a wealthy and successful merchant who had immigrated to Great Britain and built a thriving enterprise in the mercantile trade. Schwabe's eldest sister Fanny had married his closest friend, Moritz Wolff, with whom she had given birth to two sons, the eldest of whom, Gustav Wilhelm, was born in 1834. Through this association, Edward met Gustav and the two quickly became friends, sharing as they did a keen interest in ship design and the growing development of steam-propelled ships. Gustav Wolff had left Hamburg at the tender age of 14 to live with his uncle, Gustav Schwabe, in Liverpool where he attended Liverpool College to study engineering. This in turn led Wolff into an apprenticeship with Joseph Whitworth & Company of Manchester. Bright and talented, the young Gustav rapidly established a reputation as an excellent engineer and was honoured to be selected to represent Whitworth & Co. at the Paris engineering exhibition in 1855. The following year, ever keen to improve his engineering skills, Gustav joined B. Goodfellows Limited of Hyde as a draughtsman. The post would prove to be short-lived, as later in the same year he accepted a position with the Belfast shipbuilder Robert Hickson & Company as a junior manager. Gustav's move to Belfast also resulted in the rekindling of his friendship with Edward Harland.

Harland had himself arrived in Belfast during the summer of 1854 to take up the appointment of shipyard manager to Robert Hickson & Company. Hickson was essentially an iron manufacturer who knew next to nothing about shipbuilding. This fact became almost immediately apparent to the young Harland upon his arrival. Taking charge of the only vessel currently undergoing construction – an iron-hulled sailing clipper named *Khersonese* – Harland discovered that the vessel was already considerably behind schedule and long overdue for completion. The keenly observant Harland identified several areas where production of the problematic clipper could be improved and introduced new working methods to recover as much of the lost time as possible. Much to Harland's consternation, he also discovered that Hickson had been paying wages far in excess of the usual worker's wage and had accepted shoddy and inferior craftsmanship from his employees. Edward promptly slashed the wages and introduced a system of work inspection: a forerunner of today's modern quality control procedures. He also instituted a policy whereby inferior or unsatisfactory work was not only rejected, but was to be repaired or replaced at the craftsman's own expense. To further improve discipline and safety he prohibited all smoking in the workplace and on board the vessel, and demanded that no employee was to stand with his hands in his pockets for any reason whatsoever. Hickson's workers viewed Harland's methods as draconian and immediately went on strike. Without skipping a beat, Edward responded to this provocation by sacking the entire workforce and replacing them with labour recruited from Scotland. The shock tactic apparently had the desired effect.

After a suitable face-saving period of time, the striking workers grudgingly returned and accepted Harland's dynamic new policies and conditions. Unbeknown to the workforce, however, Edward Harland was facing much more serious difficulties in the financial running of Hickson's yard. Long concerned about the fiscal performance of the shipyard's operations, the Ulster Banking Company finally lost all patience with Hickson's enterprise and proceeded to foreclose on all outstanding business and personal loans in the spring of 1855. This disastrous state of affairs resulted in Edward making a risky decision to fund the daily operating costs of the yard out of his own pocket, while scrambling frantically to reach some sort of accommodation with the yard's creditors. Struggling to keep the yard in operation he unexpectedly found himself being offered some much-needed help.

Thomas Toward & Company was a long-established shipbuilding company on the River Tyne in Newcastle, where Edward had been employed for a year in 1853. Following the death of the founder, Thomas Toward, in 1855 the senior foreman, William Houston, and a large number of skilled craftsmen had moved, at Harland's request, to Belfast to help complete the now seriously delayed *Khersonese*. This influx of expert labour greatly reduced the production time and substantially increased the quality of the workmanship. Consequently, Harland was able to gain sufficient breathing space to sort out the financial mess he had inherited from Hickson.

To assist in the reconstruction of the company Edward called upon his talented friend Gustav Wolff to be his personal assistant in 1857 and together the two men assembled a rescue package for the company. Despite the numerous difficulties and tremendous pressure applied by the creditors, on 21 September 1858 Hickson formally offered Edward Harland the opportunity to purchase his entire interest in the shipyard for the then princely sum of £5,000. With his own modest finances unable to meet the offering price, but eager to avail himself of what he considered to be a golden opportunity, Edward turned to his old friend, and Wolff's uncle, Gustav Schwabe for advice and support. With Schwabe's financial backing and encouragement, Edward Harland duly purchased the entire shipbuilding enterprise of Robert Hickson on 1 November 1858, and renamed the yard Edward James Harland & Company.

Displeased with the location of Hickson's yard, Harland quickly disposed of the property and took out a lease on an area of land on the new Queen's

Island. This allowed Harland free rein to design and lay out a yard to his own exacting requirements. The Queen's Island location also provided Harland with the option for further expansion if necessary. Now in complete control of his own company's destiny, Harland appointed Gustav Wolff as chief draughtsman and charged him with reorganising the drawing offices into a more cohesive and efficient operation.

Wolff succeeded in this task to such an extent that within a few months he had, in collaboration with Edward, produced a portfolio of new and innovative vessel designs. Realising that he had discovered a kindred spirit who shared his dreams and ideals of developing modern iron steamships, Harland joined into a formal partnership with Wolff on 11 April 1861. On 1 January 1862 a new company appeared on Queen's Island: Harland and Wolff Limited. It was a name that would endure into the twenty-first century. However, nothing was certain as the two men set about the onerous task of convincing the major ship owners of the period that their innovative designs were worth considering. Harland understood that his first task would be to establish his credentials as a shipbuilder of quality and reliability by producing sturdy vessels based on tried and trusted traditional designs. So he approached an equally innovative ship owner, James Bibby & Sons Limited, with his portfolio of designs. What neither party realised or appreciated at the time was that this would sow the seeds of a long and mutually beneficial relationship.

4

A Partnership Forged in Steel

On 11 April 1861 Edward Harland and Gustav Wolff formalised their business arrangement by signing the formal Deed of Agreement that established the shipbuilding and engineering company of Harland and Wolff Limited. The partnership agreement contained some twenty-one individual clauses, perhaps the most important of which, if not the most obvious, was that 'the partners shall devote themselves entirely and completely to the business of the partnership and do nothing in connection with the enterprise without first obtaining the consent of the other in writing'.

The document was witnessed by John Bailey who had been Harland's main clerk and bookkeeper since he had purchased Hickson's yard for his own account in September 1858. Despite the agreement governing the conduct of the two partners in establishing and operating their new business, it was woefully short on any detail of how they intended to share the actual workload in running the business. While Harland, due to his previous experience, was the most obvious candidate to oversee the shipbuilding operations, it was in no manner certain that Wolff would be capable or experienced enough to control the engineering side. The situation was resolved by the appointment of William Houston, a long-time associate of Harland's who provided invaluable support to Wolff in managing the shipyard during the frequent absences of his partner in seeking new orders for the fledgling company.

In addition to the experience William Houston provided, he also offered the considerable business acumen and financial expertise of his wealthy family, an invaluable advantage not to be ignored by the embryonic business. The partnership had an established capital of £2,416, with Harland providing £1,916 and Wolff subscribing the remaining £500. While this capital base appeared insufficient to support a business with considerable future commitments – indeed, the sum was less than half the amount Harland had paid for the purchase of Hickson's shipyard alone – the partners turned to Gustav Schwabe for additional finances. Schwabe and his sister Fanny (Wolff's mother) agreed to lend the business a capital loan of £12,000, which was to be repaid out of the profits only, if any were made. The loan was granted on extremely favourable terms to the partners in that neither

Gustav Schwabe nor Fanny would have any share of the net profits generated from the business. There was a further clause, nevertheless, that neither would they be liable for any losses occurring from company operations. In line with their initial investment, the partners agreed that any profit or loss would be divided on a ratio of three to one in favour of Edward Harland. To avoid any disputes between the partners, they agreed that ship owner and entrepreneur James Bibby together with James Dugdale, who was a long-established friend of both the Harland and Schwabe families, would act as arbitrators in any disagreement.

Orders for new vessels started to appear, primarily due to the success of James Bibby & Sons' order for six ships which had been constructed to a revolutionary new hull design and provided a greater speed and stability than hitherto had been thought possible. Based on a concept first developed by Edward Harland while an apprentice, this new hull form comprised a slender contour blended with increased length. The result was a faster, more stable vessel with a greater cargo capacity than any other vessel of a comparative tonnage. This innovative combination of speed and economy proved most attractive to ship owners more used to operating conventionally designed tonnage, and as a result Harland and Wolff found themselves receiving abundant enquiries for vessels of this new design. However, this increase in enquiries proved to be a double-edged sword as the partners quickly found that the rapid success of their enterprise was leading to problems on the financial side. Having accepted what was considered a huge order from T. & J. Brocklebank for two 1,300-ton ships, together with numerous additional orders from James Moss & Company and British Shipowners Limited, the problem arose of paying for the vessels' building materials.

Although the early contracts had generated healthy profits and had seen Edward Harland's share of the business rise to almost three times his initial investment, the capital had been ploughed back into the business. Wolff, who had seen an even better return on his £500 stake, now had a stockholding valued at just over £4,500. Despite this surfeit of apparent riches, much had been used from the profits to repay the loans of Gustav and Fanny Schwabe, leaving the partners with reduced working capital to fund the new orders.

To resolve this critical situation, Harland devised a novel solution which meant these new orders would be financed by bills of exchange drawn on Harland and Wolff and accepted by the customer. This simple device provided the customer with a fixed period of credit at an agreed rate of interest; in effect, it was an early form of lease/hire purchase arrangement and was widely accepted in business as a convenient method of purchasing large items of equipment. It was Harland and his business acumen that applied it to major capital purchases such as ocean-going vessels. These bills of exchange were often agreed at a fixed rate of interest, usually 1 per cent over the Bank of England base rate, and were repayable in full at the end of the agreed term. The advantage to all parties was that these negotiable securities would be repaid normally about six months after the expiry date of the original contract; however, in exceptional cases this could be extended to some eight or ten years after expiry. The advantage to Harland and Wolff was that these instruments could be held as security until fully repaid or, more importantly, could be used as collateral for additional loans through the various financial institutions primarily in the City of London.

Alternatively, these bills of exchange could be redeemed for cash at a reduced rate from the many discount houses and banks willing to accept them. Being secured as a first charge on the vessel concerned they were considered a safe means of security, especially as the necessary insurance premium on the vessel was inevitably secured in favour of the bill holder. In the normal course of events, these bills would only ever be exchanged for a discounted rate of cash if the ship owner was experiencing particularly difficult circumstances. In all cases it was more beneficial to allow the bills to run for their full term rather than opt for what would be a considerable financial loss to cover a short-term funding shortfall. Of course, Harland and Wolff would have preferred to be paid in cash by the ship owners for their vessels, but as the size of vessel increased, so did the cost of construction, and the novel financing arrangements offered by the partners proved hard to resist. Irrespective of whatever method of payment was agreed, the construction of the vessel was paid for in instalments known as milestones. The first tranche was usually paid after the successful laying of the keel; the second when the framing had been finalised; the third on completion of the hull plating; and the final instalment was made on handover of the vessel to the owner after sea trials had been carried out satisfactorily.

The growing success of the business had not gone unnoticed by a pupil at the prestigious Belfast school, the Royal Belfast Academical Institution, otherwise known as Inst. This exclusive school for young gentlemen had a well-established reputation for producing scholars of exceeding ability, in particular engineers and architects. One such pupil was William James Pirrie, who badgered his widowed mother – William's father having died in 1849 – into arranging for him to be accepted by Harland and Wolff as a 'gentleman apprentice'. Pirrie's mother eventually gave in to his entreaties and duly arranged for William to commence his apprenticeship with Harland and Wolff on 23 June 1862. It was to be the start of a long and eventful career which would culminate in him becoming chairman of the company and more importantly establishing it as the finest shipbuilder in the world.

Despite the successful entry of Harland and Wolff on the world stage, the first years of Pirrie's employment were anything but promising. The very future of the company was thrown into doubt by a bitter dispute between Edward Harland and the Belfast Harbour Commissioners regarding the proposed siting of a new dry dock. Harland had insisted the new facility be constructed on the County Down side of the River Lagan. However, after initially agreeing to this proposal in July 1847, the Harbour Commissioners, much to Harland's chagrin and annoyance, reversed their decision in November 1862 and elected to construct it on the opposite bank of the river, but crucially without naming a location. The dispute raged on for several months more, without any apparent progress being made. The core of the argument revolved around the need to cross the River Lagan frequently and the inherent risk to life that entailed. The Harbour Commissioners argued in vain that the supposed dangers of traversing the river were overstated, but Edward Harland had the support of the powerful trade association, the Belfast Shipwrights Society, who were concerned that the loss of such a vital facility would be detrimental to the employment of their members. Buoyed by this unexpected but nevertheless welcome support, Harland forcefully argued his case that siting the new dock next to his facility could only encourage an increase in shipbuilding and repairing activity, and possibly even attract other industries to the area.

Harland was determined to brook no objection to what he regarded as essential to the continued growth of his business and, during a particularly acrimonious meeting, informed the Harbour Commissioners that if the new dock was not sited on the County Down side of the river, he would be left with no other option than to close Harland and Wolff in its entirety and relocate the company to Liverpool. Needless to say the Harbour Commissioners, horrified at the prospect of losing such an important and growing operation, quickly conceded to Harland's demands and the new dry dock was duly constructed precisely where Harland had insisted it should be. This dock became the Hamilton Graving Dock and is today the home of RMS *Nomadic*, a passenger tender to the Olympic-class vessels. As a compromise to the industrialists, however, who had argued for the dock to be built on the County Antrim side of the river, the Harbour Commissioners agreed to construct a large floating dock which many regarded as merely a consolation prize in the long-running battle for supremacy of the harbour estate and facilities. It was a battle rightly won by Edward Harland and over the coming years the conflict would reignite between the combatants on several more occasions; yet these were arguments Harland was always determined to win, and win them he did.

Never a man to underestimate, Edward Harland, by sheer force of will and his dynamic personality, dominated any discussion or debate he became involved in. By his single-minded determination to make a success of his venture he steadfastly refused to countenance any compromise on his ambition to make the Harland and Wolff name synonymous with innovative and contemporary shipbuilding.

In his desire to develop revolutionary vessel designs he experienced a high degree of frustration with others, mainly ship owners who were understandably reluctant to invest their money in anything other than tried and trusted technology. It was by dogged persistence that he succeeded in persuading a number of major ship-owning concerns, such as P&O, OSNC and Royal Mail

Lines, to adopt the design principles he was expounding, promising greater speed and efficiency in their vessels and thus greater profitability.

This radical approach to hull form quickly became known as the 'Belfast Bottom' and comprised a long slender hull with extremely fine lines, producing a sturdy and stable vessel in all but the worst storm conditions. Among the first to adopt this new hull was Harland's old friend James Bibby, who after placing an initial order for one vessel as an experiment, quickly ordered a further series of six. Buoyed by this success, Harland and Wolff soon received orders for thirteen similar vessels of varying tonnage, all based on the innovative and ground-breaking design. However, amidst this unquestionable success storm clouds were gathering on the horizon which, if left unchecked, could spell disaster for the two partners and their business.

5

The Edwardian Era & *Titanic*

The year 1866 had begun with great promise for Harland and Wolff. The work completed to date had produced a profit of some £1,960, which, if not quite as much as was hoped for, was a profit nevertheless. Good returns were expected on two vessels under construction for T. & J. Brocklebank, to be named *Candahar* and *Tenasserim* respectively. Also nearing completion was vessel number 44, as yet unnamed, which was destined to cause the partners much anguish and despondency. When the matter was finally resolved it produced a unique and unexpected partnership which led to the building of perhaps the most famous vessel in the world: RMS *Titanic*.

Construction had progressed normally on ship number 44 until the prospective owner was forced to default on one of his instalments and consequently withdrew from the contract. This had the immediate effect of plunging Harland and Wolff into a serious debt situation, and they were left with an unfinished vessel on their hands without any prospect of a sale. To compound the issue Harland and Wolff had financed the construction to date by borrowing heavily from the Belfast Banking Company, who, after being made aware of the customer default, was pressing for repayment of the loan.

In nothing short of desperation Wolff contacted his uncle, Gustav Schwabe, for help in finding a buyer for the vessel. Fortuitously, Gustav had recently been in discussion with a prospective ship owner and quickly arranged for the two parties to meet. In the meantime, Schwabe guaranteed the debt to the Belfast Banking Company by offering his home as security. Schwabe lived in the grand and imposing mansion of Broughton Hall in Liverpool, whose value far exceeded the outstanding debt and thus was acceptable by the bank as security, thus relieving the immediate pressure on the partners.

Schwabe was as good as his word and arranged for both Edward Harland and Gustav Wolff to meet Thomas Henry Ismay, who had, with Schwabe's assistance, just purchased the recently bankrupted White Star Line. Ismay realised he quickly needed to acquire new tonnage in order to maintain the old White Star service to Australia and the gold fields of New South Wales. The almost-completed hull 44 proved to be ideal for his requirements, and, provided that Schwabe would agree to pay one-quarter of the finance in the form of a loan, the vessel purchase could be completed.

In honour of this unique arrangement it was agreed to name the vessel after the saviour of the hour; accordingly, it was named *Broughton* after Schwabe's home. The introduction of Thomas Ismay to the two partners, and the timely purchase of this vessel, was to set in motion a train of events culminating in the construction of RMS *Titanic* for the White Star Line. *Broughton* only remained in the White Star fleet for eight years, after which she was sold to William Thomas & Company of Swansea who continued to operate her successfully for several years. That company finally disposed of her in 1899 for further trading. Sadly, *Broughton* was lost with all hands in 1902 on a voyage from Hamburg to Glasgow.

The relationship between White Star and Harland and Wolff continued to grow exponentially as both companies rapidly expanded their business interests and other commercial activities. Each company invested greatly in the shares of the other and as a result White Star was able to command exclusive and very lucrative building prices for new tonnage. While cross investment in associated companies was not unusual, the particular arrangement with White Star provided a rather novel agreement for the time. Shipbuilders' normal practice was to purchase a limited number of shares in the contracting company which provided the vessel owner with capital to partially finance the initial construction costs. Accordingly, the vessel would be constructed under a fixed price agreed at the contract signing, which would include provision for any specified changes in design by the owners or additional extras. Where the arrangement with White Star differed was that the contract for any new vessel would be accepted on a cost-plus basis with an agreed fixed commission of 4 or 5 per cent on the negotiated contract price.

Unusually and uniquely, the contract cost would include all material and direct labour charges; however, no provision was made for the recovery of any overhead expenditure. The terms of the contract also included punitive penalties for late delivery and the option to refuse delivery of the completed vessel if the agreed delivery date was exceeded by three months, *force majeure* excluded. By agreeing these terms, Harland and Wolff guaranteed themselves a definable level of profit on every contract which could be used as security, or at least a valuable bargaining chip, when seeking additional finance from the banks to fund further expansion of the business. On the other hand, the company was exposed to severe and potentially disastrous consequences should it fail to deliver on time and on price. A calculated risk it certainly was, yet Edward Harland had complete faith in his abilities and that of his partner Wolff to honour the deadlines they had set themselves.

In the event, their belief in themselves and their workforce proved more than justified and the success of their novel shipbuilding contract saw a considerable increase in ship owners approaching Harland and Wolff for their new vessels. The crucial advantage for ship owners was that for the first time each vessel would have an agreed and fixed cost at the outset, allowing the ship owner to manage his operating budgets far into the future without the uncertainty of unexpected costs affecting his business.

This massive increase in business found the current shipyard facilities wanting in many respects, and in order to maintain the rate of progress, Harland and Wolff immediately commenced a programme of reconstruction of the shipyard facilities, together with the purchase and installation of the most modern and efficient machinery available. Four completely new shipbuilding slips were constructed facing into the Abercorn Basin. The former patent slipways belonging to the Belfast Harbour Commissioners on the west side of the River Lagan were purchased and the two slips amalgamated into one larger unit. On the original Queen's Island site a completely new iron foundry and blacksmith's shop were constructed, together with a new plater's shed on the banks of the Musgrave Channel. To ensure the rapid and uninterrupted supply of materials, in particular iron and steel plate, the partners constructed a general purpose vessel for their own operation. *Camel* was a 269-ton steam-powered coastal trading vessel designed and fitted with an especially strengthened hull and full-length single hatchways to safely carry the large items of machinery and plate from mainland Britain. In total these improvements to the facilities and the construction of *Camel*, over the period between 1869 when the programme of reconstruction commenced until completion in 1872, cost the partners some £30,000 and was completely funded from the company profits.

With the improved working environment came the inevitable increase in the numbers employed at Queen's Island. Most notable among the new arrivals was one Alexander Carlisle, who joined the company as a premium (paid for) apprentice. His father, John Carlisle, was the headmaster of the Royal Belfast Academical Institution, which then, as today, was one of Belfast's most prestigious schools. As a premium apprentice, whose employment was funded by his family and not the company, Alexander's career was assured over the next five years, for, upon completion of his apprenticeship, he could expect a position of management in the company. Alexander Carlisle exceeded all expectations and forged an illustrious career in the design department of Harland and Wolff, eventually rising to the position of managing director at the time of the loss of *Titanic*.

Also coming to prominence was William James Pirrie who, through his engaging personality, charisma and business acumen, had forged himself a reputation as one of the brightest young men in the shipbuilding industry. Having already travelled widely on company business, Pirrie had amassed a formidable array of business contacts and thoroughly enjoyed interacting with prominent members of Edwardian society. Pirrie worked extremely hard at fostering and maintaining such beneficial relationships, keeping an eye to the future. Greatly ambitious and extremely hard-working, Pirrie knew he was destined for greatness and one day he would come to lead Harland and Wolff into becoming the greatest and best-known shipbuilding concern in the world. However, such dreams and ideals were still some way off and much would happen before his vision would become reality.

William James Pirrie had joined Harland and Wolff as a premium apprentice in 1863 and quickly established himself as a versatile and willing student of the art of shipbuilding. He completed his apprenticeship as a draughtsman in 1869 and found himself appointed as the replacement for the highly regarded William Houston, who had been the company's main draughtsman for several years and had now been appointed as shipyard manager. While such a rapid promotion was highly unusual for someone as young as Pirrie, both partners had every faith in the young man's ability and had no hesitation in making the appointment. From the outset both Edward Harland and Gustav Wolff had determined that their policy would be to promote from within whenever possible to ensure the continuity of the skill base they were building and developing among the workforce. William Pirrie was just such an example; highly intelligent and adaptable, he had revealed from the outset of his apprenticeship a capability to absorb and retain information and to quickly grasp new concepts and designs at an early stage of their development.

In furtherance of their policy of internal development, the partners introduced a share participation scheme whereby those individuals identified as potential leaders would be offered the opportunity to invest in the company and by doing so share in the profits of their labours. Also, by being shareholders they demonstrated their loyalty and commitment to the company. Pirrie, by virtue of his driving personality, was the obvious leader of this select group and in that regard his opinion was highly sought by his compatriots. Ambitious as always, Pirrie quickly appreciated this was the ideal opportunity to gain a permanent foothold into the company and wasted no time in accepting the offer of shareholding while convincing his colleagues to do likewise.

Negotiations on the structure of this new limited company, which from the outset was to remain known as Harland and Wolff, commenced in June 1874 and, for such complex dealings, were rapidly concluded by early July the same year. Thus, in August 1874 the new partnership of Harland and Wolff Limited began official operations financed by the capital investment of £76,250 divided as follows: Edward Harland, £31,500; Gustav Wolff, £15,750; William James Pirrie, £13,000; Walter Wilson, £10,000; and finally Alexander Wilson, £6,000. As a further guarantee of obtaining future work for the fledging concern, the two original partners provided a contingency fund of £73,369 as an unsecured loan to be repaid, interest-free, within twelve months of any drawdown. Thus, with its immediate financial future secured, the new and enlarged partnership commenced the search for work to fill its now almost empty order book.

Pirrie once again found himself travelling extensively across the world promoting Harland and Wolff as a shipbuilder at the forefront of technology, and offering innovative and radical designs for all types of vessel. Determined to use every avenue to achieve his target, he relied widely on his network of business contacts so painstakingly built up over the previous years. One such contact was the well-regarded shipping entrepreneur Thomas Henry Ismay, the dynamic managing director of the rapidly expanding White Star Line.

The White Star Line – or, to give it its correct title, the Oceanic Steam Navigation Company – had been one of Harland and Wolff's earliest customers. It had ordered its first vessel, the appropriately named *Oceanic*, in 1869, continuing with additional, even larger vessels as both White Star and Harland and Wolff continued to expand. From his earliest days as Harland and Wolff's draughtsman, the young William Pirrie had cultivated a deep and lasting friendship with Ismay, a friendship that was to continue and flourish into even greater familiarity with Ismay's successor, his son Bruce.

J. Bruce Ismay proved to be every bit as dynamic as his father in developing White Star into one of the most profitable shipping companies of the day. A keen student of naval architecture he, with Pirrie's willing assistance, continued to push the boundaries of ship design, constantly looking for innovative and radical design solutions to the carriage of passengers and cargo in vessels of ever-increasing size and complexity. White Star had been one of the first shipping lines to adopt steam propulsion for its rapidly expanding fleet as opposed to the traditional sail. Such was this close personal friendship that Bruce Ismay and his wife found themselves guests of William Pirrie at a lavish dinner party at his London home, Downshire House, in the heart of fashionable Belgrave Square. Ostensibly it was a social occasion between friends; however, both Pirrie and Ismay had agreed beforehand it would be an invaluable opportunity to privately discuss the impact of the recent capture of the famed Blue Riband by the Cunard Line, White Star's greatest rival, in particular on the transatlantic route. Incensed by what he perceived as indifference shown by the press to his beloved White Star Line, Ismay determined that something had to be done to redress the balance and recapture the company's leading position on the route. While excited at the prospect of this challenge, Pirrie tactfully reminded Ismay that this would be far easier said than done.

This objective would be especially difficult as White Star had always viewed the race across the Atlantic as a vulgar aside to the normal business of sea travel. However, in capturing the Blue Riband trophy for Great Britain with the *Mauretania*, Cunard Line had fired the imagination of the general public into a patriotic fervour where there had been little cause for celebration before. Indeed, the achievements of the Cunard Line had become a matter of national interest, much to the detriment of other shipping lines. Ismay had decided that just such a situation could not be allowed to continue unchecked and so he determined that, with the assistance of his great friend William Pirrie and the shipyard of Harland and Wolff, the White Star Line would create the greatest series of passenger vessels ever seen. In this quest to produce these marvels of the age, Ismay confirmed that he had absolutely no intention of changing White Star policy: he reiterated that it was his express wish to ensure the name of White Star Line would be forever synonymous with the upper end of the transatlantic passenger market and be renowned for the elegance of its service which was to be provided in the most luxurious surroundings possible.

As the evening progressed and the two friends became more relaxed, their thoughts turned to the task of formulating a conceptual design for just such a magnificent vessel. But both men rapidly realised that to maintain a regular service across the Atlantic, at least two such vessels would be required, which in the atmosphere of enthusiasm for the project quickly became three. Spurred on by Ismay's eagerness, Pirrie speedily produced an outline specification of the requirements: each vessel would be approximately 45,000 tons; steam powered, possibly to also include a steam turbine engine; and, of course, have the obligatory four funnels to denote power and majesty. The vessels would need grand names as befitted their stature and in a moment of inspiration Ismay selected *Olympic*, *Titanic* and *Gigantic* for the trio. In the event, the name *Gigantic* was never adopted; the third vessel was named *Britannic*.

Satisfied with the evening's work, Bruce Ismay left Downshire House confident that he had formulated a strategy to wrest the mantle of prominence in the shipping world back from the Cunard Line. Pirrie, on the other hand, was left with a considerable problem: Harland and Wolff simply did not have any building slipways or dry docks large enough to accommodate the construction of such leviathans. A major difficulty it might be, but for now Pirrie was content to leave the search for a solution until tomorrow.

As Pirrie returned to his office at Harland and Wolff, his thoughts were occupied with the magnitude of the task to which he had committed the company; not only were they to design and build the greatest vessels ever seen before in the history of shipbuilding, but he had to construct a shipyard capable of accomplishing such a Herculean task.

His immediate action was to bring together his two most trusted and able lieutenants: his nephew Thomas Andrews, an outstanding young naval architect, and Edward Wilding, who was the chief draughtsman with a speciality in the complex calculations necessary to produce a safe, practical and workable design. Pirrie was particularly fond of Thomas Andrews, who was the second son of the Reverend Thomas Andrews and Pirrie's sister Eliza. Born in 1873 Thomas had always enjoyed the company of his worldly uncle and had from his earliest days displayed a keen interest in ships and shipbuilding; this had been greatly encouraged by his Uncle William who took great delight in giving his young nephew the freedom to explore the wonders of Harland and Wolff as frequently as he could. On many occasions Thomas accompanied his uncle on the regular inspections of vessels under construction and was a welcome visitor to the drawing office where he would doodle for hours alongside the draughtsmen.

Titanic's main engine under construction in the erection shop.

Edward Wilding, on the other hand, was a studious individual bordering on the pedantic, which resulted in his relationship with Pirrie being one of mutual respect, yet distant to the point of being cold. This remoteness of relationship would unfortunately lead in the latter years, after the loss of *Titanic* and the resultant death of Pirrie's adored nephew Thomas, to little disguised acrimony towards Wilding and would ultimately result in a severe deterioration in Wilding's health and his subsequent resignation from the company.

Edward Wilding was responsible for overseeing the complicated design calculations, including the basic parameters that needed to be conformed with to ensure such an enormous hull could be safely constructed. These calculations were known as Scantlings and were subsequently used by the naval architects and ship designers to produce the thousands of individual and detailed working drawings necessary to complete the final construction phase of a vessel. In the case of the Olympic-class vessels, these numbered several hundred drawings, each one personally inspected and approved by Thomas Andrews before release to the trades in the shipyard and allowing construction to commence. Sadly, due to a design flaw, which in all probability could not have been easily anticipated, RMS *Titanic*, after striking a glancing blow against an iceberg on the night of 14 April during her maiden voyage, foundered due to uncontrolled flooding of five of her forward watertight compartments. Thomas Andrews and a number of other Harland and Wolff employees were on board as part of the guarantee group and by bravely remaining at their posts (although not required to), each man perished in the disaster.

At the subsequent inquiry into the loss of *Titanic*, Wilding, as the most senior figure remaining of the design team after the loss of Andrews, faced a barrage of frequently hostile questions from the inquiry team led by Lord Mersey. A quiet and reserved individual at the best of times, Wilding found such an ordeal so unbearable that his health subsequently deteriorated and he suffered what today might be diagnosed as PTSD (Post Traumatic Stress Disorder).

Additional stress was imposed by the evident disregard shown towards him by Pirrie who, perhaps rather unfairly, held him primarily responsible for the loss of his beloved nephew due to the deficiencies revealed in the vessel's design. Wilding found the unrelenting pressure and tacit animosity shown towards him by Pirrie overwhelming and he eventually decided that he had no other option than to resign from the company he had served so loyally and well over many years. A common misconception is that Wilding was dismissed by Pirrie in a fit of pique caused by his grief over the death of his nephew Thomas. In fact, Wilding continued to work for Harland and Wolff for a number of years after the loss of *Titanic*, until his already fragile health eventually broke down and he could no longer continue in his employment.

However, long before any of these things could come to pass, Pirrie had the onerous task of creating the facilities whereby construction of these 'super ships' could take place. Since 1896, when he had taken over the reins of the company as chairman from Edward Harland, Pirrie had introduced a programme of gradual improvement in the facilities at Queen's Island. He had continued to cultivate his business contacts and proceeded to shock his fellow directors by accepting the role of Lord Mayor of the City of Belfast that same year. In accepting such a high office, Pirrie was shrewdly continuing to position himself and, by default, Harland and Wolff at the forefront of commercial and business affairs in the city. Upon leaving office Pirrie accepted a position as a Harbour Commissioner for the Port of Belfast, and by doing so ensured that Harland and Wolff would always receive preferential treatment in any future harbour developments. The urgent reconstruction of the Queen's Shipyard to accommodate the Olympic-class vessels presented just such an ideal opportunity and Pirrie set to work with a will to have the necessary work commenced as soon as possible.

Pirrie had identified the Queen's Shipyard site as ideal for the new slipways as it afforded direct access to the River Lagan and a relatively straight passageway into Belfast Lough and the sea beyond. Always fiercely steadfast in his regard for Harland and Wolff, he regarded other shipyards, in particular those in Europe, as inferior to British shipyards and was determined that under his leadership

Harland and Wolff would sit atop the pinnacle of world shipbuilding. The reconstruction of the Queen's Shipyard would be best served by the demolition of the four existing slips to be replaced by two much larger ones. These slipways would eventually be allocated numbers two and three, but during construction it was discovered that a further, much smaller slipway could be constructed on slob land at an angle of 45 degrees to the new slipways.

Always mindful of the need to maximise the potential for further shipbuilding capacity, Pirrie personally championed the construction of this additional slipway against much internal opposition. In reality, this slipway proved to be of little practical use and, as a consequence, it rapidly fell into disuse, overshadowed by its two much larger neighbours. Construction of these new slipways was not in itself enough to secure Pirrie's objective; something was missing, something that would demonstrate to the world Harland and Wolff's commitment to be the most technologically advanced and progressive shipbuilder of the times. The answer proved to be surprisingly simple and would come to be regarded as the jewel in Harland and Wolff's crown. Each of the new slipways would be equipped with the largest and most powerful cranes ever devised. They would not be just any cranes, but enormous, purpose-built gantries that would dominate the skyline of Belfast.

A reconstruction of the Queen's Shipyard, with slipways Nos 1 & 2 almost complete and ready for construction to commence on RMS *Olympic* and *Titanic*.

Several designs were submitted for evaluation with the contract eventually being awarded to Thomas Arrol & Company of Glasgow. Known colloquially within Harland and Wolff as the 'water gantries', each slipway would be surmounted by its own self-contained and independent gantry operating in tandem with the other, depicting a characteristic latticework design. Each massive gantry had an overall length of 150ft and an overall safe working height of 100ft. These massive structures were themselves topped with a set of three mobile cranes, each with a lifting capacity of 3 tons. In addition to these physical land works, the decision was taken to purchase, second-hand from Blohm & Voss shipyard in Germany, a floating crane with a lifting capacity of 250 tons to allow for the installation of heavy machinery items.

The final piece in this complex jigsaw was put into place when Pirrie managed to persuade the Board of the Harbour Commissioners to fund the construction of a giant dry dock which would be capable of taking the new vessels upon their completion. This task was accomplished in the face of considerable opposition to Pirrie and his expansion plans. Several of the Commissioners displayed personal animosity towards Pirrie, regarding him as bombastic and self-serving, chiefly because he regarded them and their opinions as subservient to the requirements of Harland and Wolff. As it happens, this assumption was probably correct: Pirrie did indeed have the power on his side and would not hesitate to wield it in any manner and whenever he thought it necessary to do so. Pirrie had correctly anticipated the opposition to his plans and had developed a two-part strategy to accomplish his aims.

The first part and possibly the most dramatic was his threat to close Harland and Wolff, by this time far and away the largest employer in the country, if funding for the new dry dock was refused. From the outset of the negotiations Pirrie had horrified both the Harbour Commissioners and the Belfast City Council by advising them that he would have absolutely no hesitation in closing Harland and Wolff and transferring the work to the mainland. Alarmed by this prospect both bodies agreed to examine various ways in which funding could be provided, quickly coming to a satisfactory proposal which Pirrie grudgingly accepted, thereby cementing the impression he was not a man to be toyed with.

The second part of the strategy saw Pirrie lobbying his contemporaries in the House of Lords at Westminster, primarily to ensure that the necessary political will would be there to provide financial support should a request for assistance be received from Belfast. Pirrie was ever the astute businessman and saw no difficulty in hedging his bets, and thus it was that construction on the new dry dock began almost immediately, and by the spring of 1911 the new facility was ready. It was named the Thompson Graving Dock in honour of the chairman of the Harbour Commissioners and is today a tourist attraction on the Titanic Trail in Belfast.

With the reconstruction of the Queen's Shipyard now complete and the commissioning of the new dry dock well under way, work could commence on the first of the Olympic-class vessels on number 1 slipway. The first keel plate for RMS *Olympic*, ship number 400, was successfully laid on 16 December 1908, followed on 31 March 1909 by that of her sister ship, number 401 RMS *Titanic*, on the neighbouring number 2 slipway. Both the keel-laying and subsequent launch of each vessel was carried out without any formal naming ceremony, as was the common practice of the White Star Line. A popular expression of the time was 'We just builds 'em and just shoves 'em in the water', White Star preferring to formally name their vessels upon completion and handover from the builders.

Buoyed by the success of obtaining the White Star order and his futuristic reconstruction of the shipyard facilities, Pirrie embarked on an accelerated programme of acquisition and expansion for Harland and Wolff, the first stage of which was the establishment of a London office on King James Street. Continually spurred on by his rivals, Pirrie was fiercely determined to continue in his quest to establish Harland and Wolff as the principal shipbuilder in the United Kingdom if not the world. His ambition was given even further impetus by the continued success of his greatest rival. Established in 1880, Workman Clark and Company had been a perpetual thorn in the side of Harland and Wolff. Founded by two former Harland and Wolff premium apprentices, the two partners had established their shipbuilding yard directly opposite that of Harland and Wolff; being very well known to the numerous Harland and Wolff clients they were in an ideal position to capture some of the business for themselves.

To add what was perceived as insult to injury, Workman Clark had recently purchased the shipbuilding business of McIlwaine and Lewis, together with their subsidiary company the Ulster Iron Works, in an audacious coup from under the nose of Pirrie. Formed in 1868, McIlwaine and Lewis had established a formidable reputation in marine engineering and was an ideal enhancement to the facilities and growing reputation of Workman Clark.

Faced with what he considered to be an intolerable situation, Pirrie instituted his radical strategies to counter these perceived threats to his ambitions. The first plank in this strategy was the rapid acquisition of shipbuilding capacity on mainland Britain by the purchase of shipyards and engineering works on the River Clyde, Mersey and at Southampton, financed in the main by major borrowings from both the banks and major shipping companies of the day, secured against shares and promissory notes drawn on Harland and Wolff. Shipyards were obtained in Liverpool, Govan and Pointhouse in Glasgow, together with ship repair facilities in London and Southampton. A large engine works was opened in Finnieston in Glasgow to complement the new engine works constructed in Belfast. The Queen's Island facilities were also further modernised and new shipbuilding yards constructed. Harland and Wolff now boasted in its Belfast headquarters four individual modern shipyards: Queen's, Victoria, Abercorn, and the newest addition Musgrave, reinforced by the largest engine-building works in Europe and purpose-built joinery, upholstery, sheet metal, and electrical manufacture and repair works.

A view over the Musgrave Channel towards the Musgrave shipyard.

Over a period of just under ten years William Pirrie had succeeded in building Harland and Wolff into his vision of a massive force in world shipbuilding. Already honoured as Baron Pirrie in 1908 for his services to the City of Belfast, he would be further rewarded for his efforts by finding himself elevated to the peerage, becoming Viscount William Pirrie in 1921. However, fate would determine that it was not to be plain sailing for Pirrie and Harland and Wolff, as the world would soon find itself plunged into war in 1914.

6

The Great War & the Depression of the 1930s

When the Great War was declared on 4 August 1914 the feeling abroad was that it would be a short conflict and in all likelihood over by Christmas. Accordingly, Lord Pirrie felt no urgency to place Harland and Wolff on a war footing, especially as he had received what he considered to be a snub to the company by the Admiralty's declared intention *not* to requisition any war materials and in particular ships from the company. Pirrie was incensed at this decision, which he regarded as fundamentally wrong and tantamount to a personal rejection to be challenged at the highest level in Parliament. It had the effect of removing the shipbuilding and engineering capacity of what was then the United Kingdom's largest shipbuilder and made no military or commercial sense whatsoever. With no Admiralty work on the order books and very little prospect of obtaining any, Pirrie believed they had been placed in a disadvantageous position. Very soon his worst fears were realised as the quantity of materials and supplies available diminished significantly, which in turn had an adverse effect on production, bringing work almost to a stop. To further complicate what was rapidly turning into an extremely difficult situation, a large number of the workforce left the company to enlist in the armed forces, convinced that their particular skills would not be needed in the war effort.

Faced with the dilemma of a shrinking workforce, departing with vital skills Harland and Wolff could ill afford to lose, Pirrie proposed that the shipyard be placed on a part-time working week of twenty hours and that work on current contracts be suspended where possible in agreement with the prospective owners. These suggestions were strongly opposed in the main by the company directors and after much heated debate a compromise was reached. All-night shift working was to cease immediately, the progress on each unfinished contract was to be examined with a view to suspending or deferring delivery, and all overtime working was to be approved only where absolutely necessary and under direct approval by the directors. Despite these moves, Pirrie and his fellow directors were determined to maintain as much work on the orders as humanly possible in an effort to keep the men employed. To this end, Pirrie, along with the Board, devised a radical plan to continue work on the thirty-two vessels currently under construction. This courageous, if foolhardy, decision succeeded in preserving the remaining workforce at approximately 18,000 men, which was a considerable drop from the almost 25,000 it had employed only three months previously in July 1914.

In an unprecedented gesture, Lord Pirrie and the Board of Harland and Wolff passed a resolution at their board meeting, held on 2 September 1914, which stated that any employee who found himself financially disadvantaged by enlisting in the armed forces was to have his wages made up to the current level paid by Harland and Wolff for their trade for the duration of the hostilities; additionally, any returning employee would receive favourable consideration for any vacancy available.

This magnanimous gesture was gratefully and deeply appreciated by all those affected and engendered an even greater spirit of camaraderie within the workforce than had previously existed. Lord Pirrie found himself regarded as not only a dynamic and visionary chairman of Harland and Wolff, but a great patriot as well. During the early months of the Great War the government concentrated on completing the contracts it already had in place with their preferred Admiralty contactors. Much to Pirrie's increasing annoyance, no attempt was made to offer shipbuilding contracts to yards that had little or no experience of constructing Admiralty vessels. Despite the Harland and Wolff shipyards in Govan having previously constructed a number of cruisers and destroyers over several years, Harland and Wolff were studiously ignored in consideration for naval work. Frustrated at what he considered a grave injustice, Pirrie decided to spend more of his time at the London office where he felt he stood a much better chance of lobbying the Admiralty and indeed Parliament in regard to the merits of Harland and Wolff in pursuance of the war effort. In this endeavour he had every confidence in his deputy and chairman of the Board of Directors, J.W. Kempster, to keep the operations back in Belfast running smoothly in his absence. Notwithstanding this vote of confidence, Pirrie would leave nothing to chance and demanded weekly reports from the various heads of department, together with a detailed financial statement of accounts, all of which were to be delivered personally each Friday by the company secretary.

Suffice to say, Pirrie's lobbying bore the required result with the award of a contract to convert ten cargo vessels into mock battleships for a special service unit devised and under the direction of Winston Churchill, then First Lord of the Admiralty. This most unusual task was precisely what Pirrie had been seeking; at last he had the opportunity to demonstrate the versatility and adaptability of Harland and Wolff, and immediately he returned to Belfast to personally oversee the completion of the work. Over 3,000 men were immediately allocated to the task of building dummy superstructures and funnels out of canvas and wood;

while a further 250 woodworkers were charged with producing dummy gun turrets. Recognising the need for these deceptions to be as realistic as possible, each false funnel was outfitted with a smoke generator to create the illusion of exhaust smoke which could be detected from a considerable distance. The vessels chosen for conversion were all general cargo vessels and as such had a much higher silhouette on the waterline than a real battleship, so it was found necessary to load each vessel with approximately 34,000 tons of pig iron and concrete ballast to produce a convincing freeboard profile. A final subterfuge in producing this 'phantom fleet' was to construct false bows and sterns which completed the illusion of a powerful and modern warship. The first vessel to undergo conversion was *City of Oxford* owned by Ellerman Lines, which arrived at Queen's Island on 30 October 1914 and was handed back to the Admiralty on 3 December 1914 as HMS *St Vincent*.

Over the succeeding months further vessels arrived in the yard to undergo the procedure and by November 1914, seven vessels were in the process of conversion. That same month saw the arrival of RMS *Olympic* for emergency repairs to her hull following an unsuccessful attempt to tow the badly damaged HMS *Audacious* to Belfast. While the hull repairs were on-going, the decision was taken to convert *Olympic* into a troopship with the result that all her luxurious fixtures and fittings were removed and placed into storage in the former timber store on Queen's Island. Meanwhile, the first of the converted vessels had been returned to the Admiralty and on 15 December were formed into the 3rd Battle Squadron under the command of the former captain of the *Olympic*, Herbert Haddock.

It had become obvious by this stage that the war would last for much longer than had been originally anticipated, which in turn would necessitate the construction of many new naval vessels. Pirrie once again placed the colossal building capacity of Harland and Wolff at the disposal of the Admiralty, but this time he was positive of a much more favourable response. Lord Fisher, a long-time confidant and acquaintance of Lord Pirrie, had recently been reappointed First Sea Lord and was a strong advocate of massive sea power. Fisher had long championed the idea of naval vessels equipped with huge guns capable of firing a projectile for several miles to bombard shore batteries or other vessels at extreme range. Fisher named these vessels 'monitors' and straight away took Pirrie into his confidence about the difficulties in constructing just such a hitherto-unknown type of vessel. Pirrie accepted the challenge with great enthusiasm and by early November had produced a rough specification and draft working design drawings. Fisher was delighted and impressed in equal amounts by Pirrie's efforts and by the end of the month had instructed Pirrie to immediately begin construction on three monitors. Priority was to be given over all other new building work and consequently a slipway at the Govan facility was cleared to allow the keel of the first monitor to be laid on 1 December 1914. The remaining pair was to be built on the Queen's Shipyard slipway previously occupied by *Olympic*; such was the massive scale of this building berth that each monitor could be built end to end on the single slipway and launched together. This was the first time such an innovative technique had been adopted and it was not without risk; however, all went according to plan and both monitors were launched without incident.

Excited by the prospect of at last obtaining a potent and powerful series of vessels, Fisher and Winston Churchill feverishly began looking for opportunities to deploy them in the most effective manner. Despite not having seen any operational service, Fisher continued to press his case for a fleet of monitors to be constructed and an initial contract was placed with Harland and Wolff for a further five to be built without delay. Added to this was a firm order for a 22,400-ton battle-class 15in gun cruiser to be named HMS *Glorious*.

Priority had been given to the completion of Fisher's monitors in what was to be an extraordinarily short building schedule. However, true to his word, Pirrie was proud to announce to the Admiralty the successful launch of the first of these vessels – a 14in gun version – on 25 April 1915, rapidly followed by two more on 29 April. Fisher was obviously delighted at the startling progress and wrote to Pirrie in fulsome terms expressing his deep appreciation of the efforts produced by Harland and Wolff. Such was his delight that Fisher revealed to Pirrie his intention to order yet more monitors, which were to be even larger than those currently under construction. Outfitted with 15in naval guns supported by a secondary armament of 9in guns, these vessels would be the most powerful afloat in any navy. As a further development of the monitor principle, a smaller class was proposed and an initial order for five such vessels was placed with Harland and Wolff as a reward for the skills and commitment they had so ably demonstrated to the monitor construction programme.

By early July 1915 all the slipways were fully occupied with a mixture of naval and commercial work, but inevitably the commercial assignments were, by necessity, relegated to secondary importance. This massive influx of naval orders had a timely and fortuitous effect on the company's financial position. In the years leading up to 1914 Harland and Wolff had found itself increasing its borrowing limits to a number of bankers. This increased indebtedness was causing considerable concern to the extent that the principal creditor, the London City and Midland Bank, requested an urgent meeting with Lord Pirrie and his fellow directors to discuss the situation. Sir Edward Holden had written to Pirrie to express his personal apprehension at the ever-increasing overdraft to which the bank was exposed and demanded that Pirrie take immediate action to normalise the state of affairs. Earlier in the year the International Mercantile Marine Company, the owners of the White Star Line which had never really recovered from the loss of *Titanic*, had been placed into receivership which caused Harland and Wolff, who were a major shareholder in the group, severe financial difficulty. Such was the uncertainty of the situation that Pirrie and his fellow directors decided the best course of action would be to dispose of the IMMC shareholding as quickly as possible so as to minimise any further loss on the investment.

Within the course of a few months the huge influx of Admiralty work had completely reversed the parlous situation of the company, which now found itself in a position of profit for the first time in a number of years. The lucrative Admiralty contracts were on a cost-plus or commission basis which permitted the shipbuilder to recover all material and labour costs to which an agreed element of profit could be added, usually in the region of 6 per cent of the total cost. This drastic upturn in the company's fortunes was a great personal relief to Lord Pirrie, but was to have consequences in the future. Badly shaken by the demands of the banks, Pirrie determined that never again would either he or Harland and Wolff be placed in such an invidious position.

Unbeknown to and certainly without the approval of his fellow directors, Pirrie opened a personal set of company account books to be held at the London office under his individual control; not even the company's finance director was to have access to these ledgers which were the only record of the true financial state of the company. Why Pirrie chose to take this radical and possibly illegal course of action is open to much speculation, but it must be recognised that his driving ambition and loyalty to Harland and Wolff was such that he could not countenance anything or anyone acting to the detriment of the company. In future, all orders placed with Harland and Wolff would be personally negotiated by him, with the contract price and terms known only to him. Understandably, the complex task of maintaining a composite record of the company's financial position was a physical impossibility for Pirrie to undertake alongside his other commitments; he desperately needed someone he could implicitly trust and rely upon to perform these duties. In this he found William Tawse, the company's chief accountant, to be the ideal candidate and without further delay installed Tawse in the London office to oversee the operation and to maintain the secret ledgers.

Under Pirrie's direction Harland and Wolff now reached an unprecedented position of financial stability; profit rose year upon year exponentially, much of which was ploughed back into the business in improved facilities or the acquisition of major shareholding in various shipping lines. In just eighteen months the company had paid off all of its bank loans and stood with a credit balance across the different banks of some £550,000 − a massive sum in 1917. Pirrie was an astute enough businessman to realise that the Great War would at some time end and inevitably bring to a conclusion the lucrative Admiralty work. Eager to ensure the company would continue to enjoy such a profitable state of affairs in the future, Pirrie persisted in seeking out ways to diversify its activities. His preferred method was to invest heavily in shipping lines, believing that by being a major shareholder in the company the shipping line would give preference to Harland and Wolff for its future tonnage requirements. Pirrie had long been friends with Sir Owen Phillips, soon to be Lord Kylsant, the chairman of the fledgling but rapidly expanding Royal Mail Line. Pirrie, in the guise of Harland and Wolff, had invested greatly in the early days of the shipping line and had been made a director in 1916. Under Phillips' direction the Royal Mail Line had developed into one of the United Kingdom's largest and most important shipping groups; however, as we shall see in further chapters it was all to come crashing down in spectacular fashion several years later.

In the meantime, Harland and Wolff continued to prosper, as did Lord Pirrie. Invited by Prime Minister Lloyd George in 1917 to become the controller general of merchant shipping, Pirrie willingly accepted on condition that he could retain his chairmanship of Harland and Wolff and his various other directorships. Lloyd George cheerfully agreed, satisfied at having got his man for this new and highly significant position in government.

Pirrie was the ideal candidate: a proven industry leader and highly influential voice in shipping circles, he was perfectly placed to guide the various factions in both the shipbuilding and shipping industries in a united manner. His first task was to persuade the trade unions that productivity in the shipyards could be improved further by integration between the various trades. To this end he formed the National Committee of Shipbuilding Employers and Trade Unions to examine the problems and identify solutions that would be acceptable to both sides. Recognising a continuing shortage of skilled tradesmen he instigated a programme of introducing the most modern and up-to-date equipment to compensate for this shortfall. He oversaw the installation of hydraulic riveting machines which could do the job faster and more accurately than the old-fashioned method of hand riveting, and championed the removal of demarcation boundaries where possible.

Of course, by adopting such a programme of change Pirrie found himself the subject of much criticism from the many factions within different aspects of the industry. Many shipyards had hoped that Pirrie would abandon the wartime adoption of the 'standard' ship design in favour of a return to freedom of design. Much to their chagrin the exact opposite was to be the case, with Pirrie forcibly and cold-bloodedly demanding the retention of this method of shipbuilding so as to maximise production throughout the shipyards. Despite the at times vehement opposition to his demands, by the end of the war years Pirrie had deservedly earned the respect of his colleagues and in doing so had increased production in UK shipyards by almost 50 per cent in the final year of the Great War.

Peace was finally declared in November 1918 and Pirrie allowed himself and the workforce a well-earned break by announcing a week's paid holiday. His last act as controller general was to formally advise all ship owners that they were now free to negotiate orders for new vessels with any shipbuilder of their choice. Under Pirrie the energy displayed by Harland and Wolff had been without precedent in the annals of shipbuilding. The company had delivered a grand total of 201,070 gross tons of merchant vessels, well over 120,000 more than any other UK shipyard. It had completed over 120 naval vessels of various types, together with a range of heavy munitions such as field guns and tanks, plus various aircraft built under licence from the Vickers and Handley Page companies. In short, it had been a magnificent example of team work, dedication and the determination of one man to achieve the impossible. The end of the Great War heralded a new dawn for Harland and Wolff, and, together with other shipbuilders, the process of replacing the immense volume of tonnage lost during the conflict was begun apace. However, this false dawn was quickly to turn into days of unemployment and despair as the Great Depression of the 1930s loomed on the horizon.

The first signs of a slowdown in new shipbuilding orders became apparent in early 1925. Ship owners found it increasingly difficult to raise finance from the banks for new tonnage which in turn had a knock-on effect on the shipyards. Work continued but at a much reduced pace and previously fully occupied building slips increasingly lay idle, festooned with weeds and a general air of neglect. Pirrie, mindful of the coming storm, battled to reduce costs wherever and whenever he could in the hope of attracting what little shipbuilding or engineering work was available. Forced to start laying off some of the workforce, Pirrie desperately sought ways to attract work to Harland and Wolff, but behind the scenes he was fighting another, more critical situation. Many of the orders for new tonnage had been accepted by Harland and Wolff on the basis of long-term loan agreements secured on share capital held in the shipping companies placing the order. This situation was all fine and good provided the share value remained stable to guarantee the amount of the capital advanced.

With the global downturn in commerce, shipping companies had seen their freight rates and volume of business fall to a previously unknown low, resulting in a considerable depreciation in their share values. Harland and Wolff, itself a major shareholder in one of the largest shipping conglomerates – Royal Mail Lines, found itself uniquely exposed and vulnerable to this dire state of affairs. Lord Kylsant, the line's chairman, found himself rapidly running out of time to keep his business afloat in the face of the mounting crisis. He had paid for ships with shares drawn against the book value of various shipping lines which comprised the Royal Mail group; now the creditors were demanding the value of these shares be redeemed for cash, giving Kylsant absolutely no time or opportunity to raise alternative capital to avert disaster. It was a futile struggle and the Royal Mail Line and its subsidiary companies subsequently collapsed in 1929, causing seismic ripples across both the shipping and shipbuilding industries.

By the winter of that year things were exceedingly bleak both for Lord Kylsant and Harland and Wolff, to the extent that if no solution to the problems could be found Harland and Wolff itself could become insolvent. Kylsant, with Pirrie in support, embarked on a frantic search for help from any quarter. The banks were not interested so in desperation Kylsant turned to both the United Kingdom and Northern Ireland governments, to be met with what could only be regarded as indifference by the then Chancellor of the Exchequer. Faced with such a despairing state of affairs, Kylsant accepted it was only a matter of time before it was discovered that his Royal Mail group had been operating insolvent for some considerable time and that complete failure of the group was inevitable. In an attempt to mitigate the damage, Kylsant resigned as quickly as possible as director of his associated companies, such as Harland and Wolff. However, the rapid defection from business of such a high-profile figure in the City of London only served to cause further panic in the share markets.

It would eventually be brought to a conclusion when, on 13 May 1931, Lord Kylsant and his Royal Mail Lines auditor, Harold Morland, were arraigned at the Royal Courts of Justice in London on a charge of corporate fraud under the Larceny Act of 1861. They were accused of conspiring on dates unknown to issue a false share prospectus. Each was found guilty of fraud with Kylsant receiving a sentence of twelve months' imprisonment; Morland was required to serve four months. While the Royal Mail group scandal raged around him, Pirrie sought to keep as much of the ignominy as far away as possible from both himself and Harland and Wolff; he therefore busied himself with the urgent task of rescuing Harland and Wolff from the financial abyss it was facing. Inevitably, the stress of the affair together with his tremendous workload began to take its toll on Pirrie's health. No longer a young man he continued to work at a pace which many of his juniors would find hard to maintain and in an effort to once again fill the order books for the shipyard, in April 1924 he embarked on an arduous business tour to South America. He became very ill at the beginning of June and subsequently passed away on 6 June 1924, his body being returned to Belfast on his beloved *Olympic*.

7

Bust to Boom Once Again

Between the tragic loss of Lord Pirrie and the coming furore of the trial of Lord Kylsant, the business of keeping Harland and Wolff afloat had rested on the shoulders of Lord Kylsant himself, but it was patently obvious that this unsatisfactory state of affairs could not continue. Preoccupied with his own troubles, Kylsant had left the day-to-day running of the company to his fellow directors; this led to bitter internecine rivalry which in itself had a further damaging effect on business. The company once again needed a strong and focused leader to take charge and return Harland and Wolff to its former glory; within the ranks stood just such a charismatic figure.

Frederick Rebbeck was born in 1877 in Swindon, Wiltshire, the only son of a local farmer. He had taken up an engineering apprenticeship rather than follow his father in working the land. Upon completion of his apprenticeship he was employed by a number of companies, before arriving at Harland and Wolff's engine works in Glasgow in 1910. Frederick quickly impressed his superiors by his ability to undertake various difficult tasks and was promoted to chief engineer and head of the engine works in 1926. He then transferred to Belfast to take up his position on the main board of the company where he continued to impress his counterparts and, perhaps more importantly, the numerous creditors of the company who desperately sought a safe pair of hands into which they could entrust their considerable financial exposure. Since the death of Lord Pirrie and the collapse of the Royal Mail conglomerate, the finances of Harland and Wolff had been largely controlled by a committee of its bankers and main creditors, who had formed themselves into a broad coalition known as the Bankers Industrial Development Company; it was this influential group who believed they had found the perfect individual to lead Harland and Wolff out of the doldrums. Two of the leading figures in this group – Sir William McLintock and Arthur Maxwell – decided to approach Rebbeck on the issue and if, as they hoped, he was amenable to their proposal, would offer him the financial backing to take complete control of the company Negotiations were conducted in extreme secrecy so as not to destabilise an already tense situation among the creditors and company directors. Despite Frederick Rebbeck having no practical experience of shipbuilding, McLintock and Maxwell considered him the ideal candidate and were extremely confident they could quickly teach him the rudiments of controlling the complete operation. Buoyed by their faith in him, Rebbeck accepted their offer of support and in 1930, after purchasing the majority shareholding formally held by Lord Kylsant, officially took control of Harland and Wolff as chairman and chief executive.

The new appointment was widely accepted among the committee of creditors, with the chairman of the Belfast Banking Company, David McKee, going as far as announcing in the press that 'The appointment of Frederick Rebbeck as Chairman of Harland and Wolff will give his many friends in Belfast and the current shareholders in the company every satisfaction that a man of great experience will once again lead this magnificent company to ever greater success in the years to come'. Such fulsome praise was well deserved; by this time Rebbeck had been with Harland and Wolff for some time and had been a particular acolyte of Lord Pirrie.

The first and most important task facing Rebbeck upon taking control of the company was to institute a complete and searching review of the business, in particular its parlous financial state and the distribution of the facilities. From the outset it was abundantly clear that Harland and Wolff, as it stood, was haemorrhaging cash at an alarming rate. Vast amounts of debt remained unpaid while at the same time huge amounts of credit was outstanding to the company from various shipping lines who hadn't paid off their accounts; by far the largest of these was the Royal Mail Line. Horrified at what was being discovered, Rebbeck wrote in despair to the heads of the leading banks, pleading for some leeway in his

Sir Fredrick Rebbeck.

restructuring of the company and especially its finances. In doing so Rebbeck was taking a calculated risk that the banks would support him, at least for the foreseeable future; he reasoned that it would not be in their interest to see Harland and Wolff become bankrupt and as a consequence see their loans wiped out at a stroke.

By early August 1930, Rebbeck had completed his review of the business and at a board meeting on the 7th he presented his findings to a shocked and dismayed group of directors. His directives would prove to be radical and uncompromising in the extreme, but were absolutely vital if the company was to continue. His first instruction was that the ship repair operations currently covering three sites – Belfast, Glasgow and Southampton – would be merged under one management structure and controlled directly from Belfast. On the shipbuilding operations his directive was bordering on the brutal: twelve of the forty-two building slipways would be closed immediately and the machinery sold. Two satellite shipyards – Caird's in Glasgow and the Harland and Wolff yard at Meadowside, also in Glasgow – were to be closed after completion of any work in hand and offered for sale. The ship repair facility in London was also to be closed with immediate effect. On the financial side, an immediate exercise to recover all outstanding debts from ship owners was put into operation, with the threat of severe interest penalties should any further delay be experienced.

As a further safeguard to Harland and Wolff's exposure to the debt due from the Royal Mail Line, of which Harland and Wolff still retained a major and significant shareholding, Rebbeck obtained a written guarantee from the administrators that Royal Mail Line would not seek to obtain tenders for any further vessels without first reference to Harland and Wolff. Rebbeck demanded this written assurance because he was concerned that rival shipyards, mindful of the predicament in which both the Royal Mail Line and by default Harland and Wolff found themselves, would offer unrealistic contract prices simply to obtain a foothold in what had been up to now a private arrangement between the two companies to the exclusion of all others. Rebbeck certainly was not afraid of competition and he had enough knowledge of the pricing structure of vessels to ensure that he would be able to detect an artificially low bid for any vessel. Harland and Wolff may be in financial difficulty, but Rebbeck fully realised that tendering unrealistic or uneconomic prices was not the way to resolve its problems. The vultures may be circling but Rebbeck demanded a level playing field; in this he received the support of the banks who were placated in their anxiety by Rebbeck's assurance that they were welcome to examine the accounts in forensic detail for every vessel tendered for by the company.

Amidst this turmoil a surprising development took place on 17 September when William Strachan, the chairman of the also financially troubled Workman Clark Shipyard, called on his banker Frederick Hyde, head of the Midland Bank, to enquire if a merger between Workman Clark and Harland and Wolff would be possible. The Depression had hit Workman Clark especially hard and in 1928 William Strachan and his brother James had effectively remortgaged the company, but with little success. It had continually struggled to find work and was facing the ever-increasing spectre of closure. Selling out to Harland and Wolff would, if it could be accomplished, at least save some of the skilled workforce from inevitable unemployment.

Hyde at first was sceptical that such an arrangement was possible given the current position of Harland and Wolff, but he agreed to put the idea to Rebbeck as the very least he could do. Understandably, Rebbeck did not appear to welcome the proposal; he was still completing the drastic reconstruction of Harland and Wolff and therefore was in no doubt that to enter negotiations at such a delicate time would not be supported by the Board of Directors. He nonetheless reported the approach he had received from Hyde and, as he anticipated, received a negative reaction from the Board. Nevertheless, the matter was officially noted and while not completely ruled out at this time, a formal decision would be deferred until a more favourable time.

Rebbeck's reticence on the issue was completely understandable: he had just restructured the company in a remarkably short period of time with the result that the order book appeared healthier than at any time since the wartime explosion of orders for replacement tonnage. Yet the downside was that these new orders had to be accepted on stringent financial terms which allowed very little to no room for overrun in expenditure.

The seemingly prosperous order book in fact masked a very serious position for the company. Cash in hand at the bank was nearly depleted with almost no reserves to be called upon. Advance payments placed by two major shipping lines had been withdrawn as the contracts could not be fulfilled, which in turn further depleted the cash resources.

Rebbeck once again found himself and the company facing a financial brick wall in that by the end of September 1930, the bank overdraft stood at £2,163,700 – a massive jump of some £250,000 in two months. Faced with such a liquidity crisis, Rebbeck was forced once again to throw himself on the mercy of the banks. Again, the choice was stark: pump more cash into the company or it would have no other option than liquidation. Rebbeck needed an immediate cash injection of £250,000 by the end of October in order to meet the wage bill and pay the accounts due; unfortunately, the entire capital of Harland and Wolff stood at only £45,000 and that was only available as an overdraft. The chance of Rebbeck obtaining just such a lifeline was slim: the Wall Street Crash had seen shipping rates and the subsequent price that could be negotiated for new tonnage slashed to unprecedented low levels; shipyards were chasing already harassed ship owners for orders for which there was simply no demand, with the result that both shipping and shipbuilding had entered a vicious downward spiral that nobody could predict the bottom of.

In an effort to appease the banks and cut even further the operational costs of Harland and Wolff, Rebbeck found himself having to close the Scotstoun yard, abandon any hope of reopening the London works and lease part of the Southampton repair facility as a warehouse. On the whole the banks were amenable to Rebbeck's proposals, but determined that even more, drastic cuts should be made. The future of the yards on the River Clyde came under discussion and the long-term view was that they should be progressively run down as the work in hand was completed. For the moment the Pointhouse yard was considered suitable for 'mothballing' until such times as an upturn in shipbuilding work could be anticipated. Rebbeck's plan was reluctantly accepted by the Board and implemented without any further delay, with the result that the workforce found itself gradually reduced as contracts were completed. The yards eventually closed one after another.

Rebbeck's draconian strategy had the desired effect and the necessary financial lifeline was provided once again with the support of the banks; however, it was not entirely due to the strenuous efforts of Rebbeck. Frederick Hyde in particular had been keenly aware of the need to maintain the active support of the government of Northern Ireland in the rescue operation; his bank was, after all, the major creditor to Harland and Wolff with loans and overdrafts currently in excess of £3 million. The Stormont Parliament fully appreciated that the demise of Harland and Wolff would be nothing less than a major industrial disaster which was to be avoided at all costs.

At the root of Harland and Wolff's problems lay the debacle of the Royal Mail Line and in November 1930, after the banks had once again pumped massive amounts of cash into the company, it became apparent to even the most casual observer that something drastic had to be done to separate Harland and Wolff from the albatross around its neck that was the Royal Mail Line. To conceive a final resolution to this festering sore a tripartite group, comprising the banks, the Treasury and the Northern Ireland government, was established. Rebbeck, much to his chagrin, was told his input would not be required. The group's first action was to agree a moratorium on the Royal Mail Line's loan repayments for a further year, until the end of December 1931. However, it neglected to advise the remaining shareholders in the Royal Mail Line of this arrangement, resulting in much anger and dismay at what they considered to be rather high-handed action by an unelected body. Much smoothing of ruffled feathers took place over the next few months and by March 1931, at the Annual General Meeting of the Royal Mail group, the resolution was grudgingly passed by the shareholders.

Rebbeck now found himself free from the dead weight of Royal Mail and viewed the future as nothing but positive. He had been handed a relatively clean slate: the shareholders in Harland and Wolff had professed every confidence in him and he in turn had promised them that a return to profitability was assured. It could be said that Rebbeck was perhaps 'gilding the lily' by making such positive pronouncements. The situation for shipbuilding was desolate and he had absolutely no grounds for such optimism, but his rhetoric was precisely what the shareholders needed and wanted to hear, and as such he carried them with him in his enthusiasm. There *was* work out there, all he had to do was find it – perhaps more simply said than done – but at least the road ahead was now clear.

Rebbeck had a lavish brochure produced illustrating the modern shipbuilding facilities enjoyed by Harland and Wolff, with great emphasis being placed on its past record of building some of the world's most luxurious and magnificent vessels. He sought ways to diversify into other areas of engineering and managed to obtain a contract from the Buenos Aires Great Southern Railway for a series of diesel-electric locomotives. But Harland and Wolff quickly discovered that there were enormous difficulties in designing and building a successful class of locomotive and the project was not continued with.

The year 1932 opened with gloomy prospects and Rebbeck once again found himself faced with considerable financial restraints. The working capital of the company had been restricted to just £100,000, and worse news was to come when once again the moratorium of payments due from the Royal Mail Line was extended by a further three months. By this time Rebbeck had despaired of ever seeing the outstanding debt settled and decided to confine his future planning for the company on the basis that these debts would be written off in their entirety.

Faced with such uncertainty Rebbeck had no other option than to issue the shareholders with a negative projection for the future. He was compelled to forecast considerable losses for the coming financial year of at least £108,000, rising to £137,000 in 1932 and £142,000 in 1934 unless an unexpected upturn in the shipping market could be realised. Faced with such a dire forecast the shareholders demanded even more: immediate cuts to the company's overheads, together with a renewed programme of savings to be implemented with the utmost speed. Rebbeck knew in his heart that further reductions to the workforce would mean that Harland and Wolff could no longer be viable as a major shipbuilding operation; yet faced with such a mauling by the shareholders he had to at least be seen to go through the motions of making further cuts across the board.

Foremost in Rebbeck's mind was the knowledge that all orders currently being tendered for were being quoted at uneconomic and unprofitable prices, something that Harland and Wolff simply could not contemplate doing and which was tantamount to financial suicide. Faced with such a pessimistic outlook, Rebbeck feared the worst and once again opted for further closures of some of the smaller shipyards in the Harland and Wolff group. He was determined at any cost to keep the operations in Belfast as intact as possible, fearing that if the nucleus of the company succumbed to closure, it would never reopen. Instead, he embarked on a sequence of planned closures of the mainland facilities in order to preserve the core workforce in Belfast. During this difficult exercise further misery would be heaped upon his shoulders, when the High Court in London pronounced on 24 June 1931 that the moratorium on the Royal Mail Line debts would be extended for a further three years, until 31 December 1934. While not unexpected it was another blow to Rebbeck and his financial strategies to keep Harland and Wolff afloat. Rebbeck knew he had to regroup his ideas, beginning with a radical overhaul of the existing Board of Directors, many of whom had been in place since the days of Lord Pirrie, and found the current situation far removed from the heady days of the past.

Rebbeck realised that the financial operation of the company needed drastic overhaul for at least a fighting chance of success. The Midland Bank, as the major creditor, was given a seat on the Board together with another nominee representing the government of Northern Ireland. Of the current directors, Lord Pirrie's faithful chief accountant, William Tawse, was offered early retirement, as was Saxon Payne. Replacing Tawse was Frederick Spark, formerly of Price Waterhouse, the company's auditors. A lifeline was thrown to the new Board by the Midland Bank offering to increase the capital limit from £100,000 to £200,000 on condition that any new orders would be secured at a profitable price and that the company could show further substantial reductions in overhead expenditure.

Rebbeck's financial forecast for the next two years proved to be uncannily accurate, with the last launch of any vessel from the shipyards of Harland and Wolff taking place on 10 December 1931, when the motor vessel *Highland Patriot* took to the water. For the next three years the slipways at Harland and Wolff lay empty and derelict as the economic recession continued to exercise its grip on the nation. Outfitting and general repair work had also dried up with the departure of the White Star liner *Georgic* on 10 June 1932. It was not until 1 May 1934 that the Shaw Savill cargo ship became the first vessel to be launched at Queen's Island once again.

During these barren years the primary staff had not been idle: many new vessel designs had been produced, introducing more efficient and cost-effective hull forms which attracted much interest from ship owners keen to reduce their costs as much as possible. The technical staff, together with the accounts office, had devised a completely new method of cost control based on a centralised contract and buying department. Of course, it was not all good news: the number of tradesmen required for shipbuilding operations had been completely decimated with the result that unemployment in Belfast in 1932 had climbed to over 76,000, representing a staggering 28 per cent increase in the year. This startling amount is brought into even sharper focus when the figures for shipbuilding and engineering are taken in isolation. Around 68 per cent of the workforces previously employed in this industry were now unemployed, with many relying on the system of Outdoor Relief payments for basic survival. Paid at a flat rate of 16 shillings per week *per household*, many found themselves on the brink of starvation. Unrest festered unchecked among the disaffected masses, erupting in an outbreak of rioting on 3 October 1932, which saw two people lose their lives in scenes of violence over several days. The situation could not be allowed to continue and in February 1934 the Ministry of Finance of the government of Northern Ireland agreed a fiscal package to underwrite Harland and Wolff in tendering for any shipbuilding orders available.

This had an immediate and positive effect on the company: freight rates had already shown signs of recovery in late 1933 and ship owners were becoming cautiously optimistic for the future. Rebbeck considered that this was the ideal time to relaunch Harland and Wolff, armed as it was with a bulging portfolio of new and innovative designs. Rebbeck's confidence was well founded and the order book rapidly began to fill once again to the extent that by 1 March, Rebbeck was able to report to the Board that orders for some fifteen vessels had been secured. This figure was increased to twenty-four vessels by July of that year.

Once again the sights and sounds of shipbuilding returned to Queen's Island as every available building berth was occupied by hulls undergoing the various stages of construction. Rebbeck had weathered the storm and emerged with a more vibrant Harland and Wolff. He also enjoyed the confidence of the workforce who had seen him rescue their jobs and livelihoods from the edge of disaster.

The Board of Directors regarded him as the new Lord Pirrie after almost single-handedly dragging Harland and Wolff back from the brink of failure, but it was the banks that were most impressed by the turn of events. Whatever magic Rebbeck possessed was working and so they were content to let him carry on doing whatever he wanted. They were in this with Rebbeck for the long term and were content to wait for the day when Harland and Wolff would start repaying the debts it owed to them. Rebbeck took a more pragmatic view, however; the contracts Harland and Wolff had secured were at an extremely low price with little margin for profit, but he wanted as much of it as he could get and would grind out a return however small.

The mood of almost euphoria in the yard was dampened on 17 June 1935 by the death of Lady Pirrie, who had held the honorary position of company president since the loss of her beloved husband. Lady Pirrie, despite her declining health in the latter years of her life, had always displayed a keen interest in the fortunes of Harland and Wolff, and had made a tradition of providing all the senior managers of the company with a personal gift at Christmas. Lady Pirrie was laid to rest beside her husband in Belfast City Cemetery at a ceremony attended by all the directors and senior managers of Harland and Wolff.

With the upturn in Harland and Wolff's prospects, the proposal to acquire the business of the Workman Clark shipyard once again came to the fore. For many years Rebbeck had viewed the presence of Workman Clark in the Victoria Shipyard on Queen's Island as a boil he desperately wanted to lance. Occupying as they did a large chunk of Queen's Island right in the middle of Harland and

Wolff, the situation was intolerable to Rebbeck who had long envisioned the whole of Queen's Island as firmly Harland and Wolff territory.

Negotiations had dragged on in a half-hearted manner for some years, with neither side displaying any sense of urgency; but matters had now come to a drastic head for Workman Clark. The depression in shipbuilding had hit Workman Clark even more severely than Harland and Wolff, with only one vessel being completed in the three years since 1931. During the intervening years it had struggled by on meagre repair work, until in February 1935 all the remaining workforce was dismissed and the yard placed on an ad hoc basis. The assets, such as they were, were placed in the hands of the receiver for disposal and by April 1935, Harland and Wolff had agreed in principle the purchase of the Workman Clark business in exchange for their shareholding in the shipyard of D. & W. Henderson of Glasgow. It was a logical and fortuitous step for Rebbeck because at a stroke he had gained control of the entire Queen's Island site, acquired a second engine works and an entire repair facility in the Abercorn Basin.

The future for Harland and Wolff, while not yet fully assured, had certainly taken on a much brighter outlook and yet once again the storm clouds of war were on the horizon. Rebbeck, ever mindful of the years of prosperity the Great War had produced, was keen to position the company at the forefront of any possible munitions work. Supported by the Admiralty, Rebbeck approached the Belfast Harbour Commissioners with the proposal to construct a new outfitting

Ships really do have wings – the fin stabiliser on *Pendennis Castle*.

berth with a 300-ton capacity crane to enable the shipyard to undertake the refitting of battleships. Grudgingly, the Harbour Commissioners gave their approval to the work which involved the amalgamation of the first two outfit quays on the Musgrave Channel. Time was of the essence to ensure the facility was ready for the launch of the aircraft carrier HMS *Formidable*, scheduled for the end of 1939. However, events were to move rather quicker than Rebbeck had

The stabiliser is retracted but note the ramshackle staging arrangement – shipbuilding was dangerous!

Another view of Musgrave Channel.

anticipated and in September of that year, Great Britain once again found itself at war with Germany.

As the last vessel to be launched at the shipyard prior to the declaration of war, *Formidable* had a rather tragic baptism into her military career. During the launch ceremony on 17 August 1939, the fore poppets supporting the bow of the vessel suddenly collapsed, with the result that *Formidable* started to slide down the slipway before the launch party could carry out the naming ceremony. Amid much panic the huge vessel continued unchecked down the slip amid a cloud of smoke, steam and broken timber, causing the spectators to scatter in all directions. While no damage was caused to the hull of *Formidable* from its premature launch, tragically the wife of a shipyard worker, a guest at the launch, was struck on the head by a flying bolt and killed.

8

On the Front Line Again

3 September 1939 dawned clear and bright above the slipways of Harland and Wolff, which were unusually quiet because it was a Sunday, almost universally considered by the populace of Northern Ireland a sacred day of rest. One man, however, found himself feverishly pondering what this fateful day would mean to the country, and Harland and Wolff in particular. Just over twenty years ago peace had been declared in a global conflict and now, once again, the world stood on the brink of another conflagration. Rebbeck had long expected such developments and had for several months secretly worked to establish Harland and Wolff at the forefront of the inevitable munitions and supply work necessary for the war effort to succeed. Uniquely placed in Northern Ireland and therefore far away from the mainland shipyards which he rightly considered would be prime targets, Harland and Wolff was well out of reach of enemy bombers, or so he thought; however, subsequent events would prove otherwise.

Rebbeck had another ace up his sleeve in the guise of the vast pool of skilled labour in and around the City of Belfast; many of these men were still languishing on the unemployment register and could be quickly re-assimilated to either shipbuilding or munitions work, both of which Harland and Wolff were ideally suited to provide. Munitions skills honed during the 1914–18 conflict had not been forgotten and the machinery to once again produce guns, equipment and munitions could be rapidly brought back into service. As Rebbeck had anticipated, orders for new naval vessels were almost immediately placed by the Admiralty, which rapidly filled the order book to capacity. The first of these was for a series of minesweepers, together with an initial requirement for a series of Flower-class corvettes. These all-purpose vessels were a development of an earlier design of whale catcher and were vital for convoy protection work, armed as they were with anti-submarine depth charges and latterly the Hedgehog mortar system.

All shipbuilding operations in the United Kingdom were placed under Admiralty control by the beginning of October 1939, and permission would only be granted for the construction of merchant vessels as replacements for tonnage lost due to enemy action, and even then it would be to an approved standard design only. Orders for naval work were placed in unprecedented quantities and on 26 September Rebbeck received a call from Winston Churchill seeking assurance that Harland and Wolff could once again be relied upon to support the war effort in any way possible. Rebbeck had no hesitation whatsoever in providing the assurance Churchill sought and was stunned when he was awarded then and there with an order for a further twenty-four Flower-class corvettes.

The remainder of 1939 saw the arrival of more orders in the shape of six 8,000-ton oil tankers, a Dido-class cruiser HMS *Black Prince*, a further six Flower-class corvettes and three Admiralty-designed armed trawlers. As the war progressed, an ever-increasing workload fell upon the ship repair division due to damage inflicted on vessels in convoy work and the additional maintenance required on over-stressed hulls and machinery. A number of conversion contracts were also placed with this division, perhaps the most unusual being the adaptation of three Shaw Savill cargo vessels to dummy battleships – a ruse successfully developed by Churchill during the First World War. These vessels named *Pakeha*, *Waimana* and *Mamari* were taken in hand from lay-up on the River Clyde and in just two months reappeared as Royal Sovereign-class battleships: *Pakeha* as HMS *Revenge*; *Waimana* as HMS *Royal Sovereign*; and *Mamari* as HMS *Hermes*, a dummy aircraft carrier complete with a full complement of wood and canvas aircraft.

Between 3 September and 31 December 1939 an astonishing 285 vessels received attention at the company's Southampton repair facility, while Belfast completed repairs on a further 216 in the same period. This astounding throughput was achieved by the addition of some 18,000 employees, with 8,400 going to the Southampton works and the remainder to Belfast. As an additional fillip to the war effort, January 1940 saw the opening of a remote satellite site at Balmoral, on the fringes of Belfast, to construct aircraft fuselages in association with Short Brothers and Harland Ltd, the well-known aircraft manufacturer. The establishment of this production line saw the first complete aircraft being delivered to the Royal Air Force on 2 April 1940, with production continuing on various aircraft types until August 1945. Perhaps the most famous aircraft constructed at the Balmoral facility and assembled at the Queen's Island headquarters was the Sunderland flying boat, rather an appropriate type produced through collaboration between a shipbuilder and an aircraft manufacturer.

While the company had shown a small return to profitability during the latter part of 1938, the influx of new Admiralty orders had a dramatic effect on the balance sheet: profit before tax for 1939 was posted at around £800,000. The astounding upturn in fortunes was greatly welcomed by the different creditors, not the least of whom were the banks. Unfortunately, this booked profit was exactly that: a figure on the balance sheet which did not relate to actual cash in hand or available capital. This curious state of affairs derived from the Admiralty – now the only permitted customer – only paying for its vessels upon completion.

Although Admiralty contracts were extremely profitable for any shipbuilder, being offered on a cost-plus basis (all labour and material costs plus an agreed profit of 6 per cent), they required the shipyard to meet all on-going construction costs from their own reserves. With such a large volume of orders in hand, Harland and Wolff found themselves in a difficult liquidity position due to the huge amount of equipment and supplies necessary to complete the orders.

With financial guarantees from the government of Northern Ireland and support from the UK Treasury, extended lines of credit at extremely low rates of interest were made available to the company and removed the pressure on its balance sheet.

Throughout the war years Harland and Wolff continued to produce vessels of all types at an astonishing rate and were acknowledged to be the most productive shipyard in the United Kingdom. Although the shipyard was situated in the north-west of the UK, and in Rebbeck's opinion probably immune to enemy bombing raids, he was to be proven wrong on the nights of 7 and 8 April 1941, when a Luftwaffe attack struck the city, targeting the shipyard and dock areas. During the air raid large sections of Harland and Wolff were devastated, with huge fires raging in the engine works and timber sheds along the Queen's Road. As the workforce surveyed the aftermath in the morning light, a number of parachute bombs could still be seen dangling from the tangled steelwork of the gantry cranes. Work commenced immediately to repair the damage and restart production; in particular, two half-completed hulls had been blown over on the Queen's Shipyard slipways, but within three days these had been righted and work carried on apace.

The bombers returned a week later, on 15 April, to finish what they had started, but on this occasion the harbour area was spared the degree of devastation it had previously encountered: the bomber crews, confused by the sight of the water works to the north of the city, dropped their bombs in that area instead. A total of 754 people were killed in that one night, with over 1,600 houses completely destroyed and a further 32,000 seriously damaged.

The Luftwaffe were not quite finished with Harland and Wolff as aerial reconnaissance photographs revealed their error and a massive raid was planned for 4 May 1941. A force of 230 bombers pounded the shipyard without mercy for several hours and the damage to the facilities was enormous, with all power lines and water pipes severed and many of the buildings completely destroyed. Many vessels on the slipways were badly damaged, with few others escaping unscathed; yet the spirit of the workforce remained largely unbroken and they set to with a will to once again repair the destruction and carry on as normal, or as normally as possible given the circumstances. Other areas of Harland and Wolff also received the unwelcome attention of the Luftwaffe, with Glasgow, Southampton and Liverpool suffering huge blows; however, the most devastating degree of destruction was perhaps sustained by the London

Queen's Road: a typical traffic scene in the shipyard.

works, which was completely destroyed in a series of concerted air raids on the London Docklands.

The total amount of damage to the company's facilities was estimated to be in the region of £3.25 million and, as is usual in the course of such massive claims, became subject to a protracted dispute between the company and the government. Rebuilding Harland and Wolff would be another Herculean task as nearly all the infrastructure and facilities had been destroyed.

It was left to Harland and Wolff to fund this rebuilding out of its own resources, which placed an intolerable strain on the company finances; it had to turn once again to its principal banker for assistance and support. The Admiralty had approved without demur the damage claim, however the Treasury proved to be a much harder proposition and despite approval for reparation being received from another government body – the War Damage Commission – the Treasury continued to drag its heels over payment. The matter was eventually resolved on the direct intervention of Winston Churchill, who instructed the Treasury to settle the issue in full without any further prevarication.

There was another influx of orders in 1942, comprising eighteen Algerine-class minesweepers, three oil tankers and eleven merchant vessels, but despite this being good news for the order book, financially it was nothing short of catastrophic. Obtaining the necessary materials would stretch the shipyard finances to almost beyond breaking point, a dreadful situation made worse

Transporting a typical ship section past the main office block.

A floating crane lifts another load.

A floating crane installing a funnel on Alfred Holt (Blue Funnel Line) passenger cargo vessel *Ascanius*.

by the effects of the damage caused to the infrastructure of the company. This extreme financial exposure was instrumental in forcing a considerable change in the make-up of the Board of Directors in November of that year. Charles Payne accepted voluntary retirement after a loyal service spanning forty-six years, while four new directors were appointed: L.V. Dunlop was placed in charge of the Govan operation; Atholl Blair became engine works director; John Morrison took responsibility for shipbuilding operations on Queen's Island; and Frederick Spark became chief accountant. Spark's appointment marked a watershed in directorships at Harland and Wolff as this was the first time a chief accountant was permitted a seat on the Board.

Rebbeck was ecstatic at these appointments as he now commanded a Board of Directors entirely subservient to his will. Freed from the shackles of the past Rebbeck now saw the way ahead for the company to reflect his vision of the future, to build on Lord Pirrie's legacy and create a shipbuilding and engineering empire as he envisioned and in doing so establish his own place in history.

Design and innovation had always been a hallmark of Harland and Wolff-built ships and this originality of thought was rewarded in 1943 by a contract for nine Castle-class escort vessels. These were a development of the successful Flower-class minesweeper, with twin propellers, much larger fuel tanks allowing greater range to cross the Atlantic without the need to refuel, and much better armament. Perhaps a more welcome improvement was the provision of better accommodation for the crew, with increased living spaces and an enlarged galley for the service of hot food at all times. Of course, the capacity of Harland and Wolff to produce major warships was not overlooked and alongside these smaller vessels, two huge aircraft carriers dominated the skyline of Queen's Island.

The Hermes-class carriers HMS *Centaur* and HMS *Bulwark* were rapidly taking shape, although due to their complexity of design and massive size neither would enter service until the war had ended. Construction time had been greatly reduced due to the introduction of electric welding as opposed to the old-fashioned riveting for hull construction. Production times were decreased by a factor of almost 50 per cent which may be best illustrated by the fact that the construction of a Flower-class minesweeper was completed in just ten weeks from keel-laying. Rebbeck, now Sir Frederick Rebbeck, having been knighted in 1941, continued to drive the company forward to even greater feats of shipbuilding and engineering. Often seen prowling the corridors of the company, usually with his jacket removed and trouser braces lowered off his shoulders so they dangled from his hips, nothing escaped his eye for detail. Prone to walking at a brisk pace, 'Old Sir Fred', as he was affectionately called but *never* to his face, was a common if feared sight as he charged along seeking out some hapless individual who had somehow incurred his wrath. A popular if apocryphal tale relates to Sir Fred looking out of his office window only to spot a number of workers attempting to slip away from work by lowering themselves out of a window. Enraged by such behaviour Rebbeck charged across the Queen's Road and administered a severe kick to the backside of one luckless individual; whether true or not this anecdote ably illustrates the irascible nature of Sir Frederick Rebbeck.

The remainder of the war years continued in much the same vein as the previous three and eventually, by the time peace was declared in 1945, Harland and Wolff had established a reputation for quality and dependability. The feeling among the workforce was of a difficult job well done, and both the management and workforce allowed themselves to bask in a record that was second to none. According to the Admiralty records, Harland and Wolff from September 1939 until April 1945 had produced an astounding 147 naval vessels, including four aircraft carriers, two cruisers, twenty-nine minesweepers, forty-seven corvettes and nine frigates, together with over 130 landing craft of various sizes. On the merchant side the company had delivered some seventy-six cargo vessels with a combined tonnage of 610,345, which included no less than thirty-two oil tankers. However, work in the shipyard was not simply confined to building ships; war work also included the production of artillery pieces, tanks and aircraft fuselages, and the repair or overhaul of over 22,400 ships. Sir Frederick Rebbeck had rightfully established himself as every bit a giant in the shipbuilding industry as Lord Pirrie had been, albeit under different yet uncannily similar circumstances. His dictatorial and at times overbearing nature had not endeared him to many people, yet he had successfully steered Harland and Wolff through the most

Fitting the main engine
before testing.

Thompson Wharf in the early
1960s.

difficult period in its existence. Much of the Blitz damage had been repaired
and most of the worn-out equipment already replaced; Rebbeck was now
indisputably in control of Harland and Wolff and could look towards the future
with a mix of confidence and faith, believing he had placed the company in the
best possible position to reap the rewards of peace.

Installing a boiler at the outfit quay.

A funnel leaving the boiler shop.

Hard at work building the best.

Many hands make light work of installing a funnel.

Just another typical day at the outfit quay.

An interesting postscript to the history of Harland and Wolff during the war years would be the debate over a contract received in 1942 for an Ark Royal-class aircraft carrier. Originally designated as an Audacious–class aircraft carrier, this was amended to Ark Royal class by 1942 when final design work had been completed. The first and therefore name vessel of the class was to be HMS *Ark Royal* and was ordered to be built by Cammell Laird & Company of Liverpool. The original order called for four vessels, however two were subsequently cancelled before construction could commence. The second vessel was ordered from Harland and Wolff originally under the name HMS *Audacious*, however this was subsequently amended to HMS *Eagle*. These superlative vessels were designed as the largest aircraft carriers ever to be built for the Admiralty, with Cammell Laird having the responsibility for all design work. Being the lead yard of the class, they would provide Harland and Wolff with the necessary construction drawings, for both vessels were to be identical; and in that lies the tale. When the hull lines' drawing was obtained by Harland and Wolff an error was made by the mould loft staff which resulted in the measurement being taken from outside the shell plating rather than inside. This minor miscalculation resulted in HMS *Eagle* being slightly wider by the margin of two thicknesses of hull plate and having a slightly greater deadweight, making her the larger of the two sister ships. While this tale may again be apocryphal, it has endured throughout Harland and Wolff's history and has become part of the folklore surrounding the company.

9

Happy Days Are Here Again: the '50s & '60s

I n the immediate aftermath of the Second World War every shipbuilder in the United Kingdom found itself ideally placed to pick and choose from a welter of orders for new vessels. All the major ship owners urgently needed new tonnage to replace those vessels lost over the past five years and naturally Harland and Wolff was in the vanguard of shipyards eager to fill its order book. Admiralty work had disappeared almost overnight; however, what orders remained had their delivery dates postponed as almost continual modifications to the specifications were received from the Admiralty. While this served to occupy a large section of the workforce, it did not occupy all the available labour and therefore some new orders needed to be secured as a matter of urgency if the workforce, now numbering an impressive 62,000 on Queen's Island alone, was to be retained. As previously seen in 1918, the cessation of hostilities produced a boom time in new orders with no less than twenty-three vessels being ordered in 1946, many of them large passenger/cargo liners. Prominent among these was the Royal Mail Line *Magdalena*, which would bring echoes of RMS *Titanic* once more to Harland and Wolff. Built for the South America trade, *Magdalena* was a 17,547-ton passenger/cargo liner launched in Belfast on 11 May 1948 and delivered to her owners on 18 February 1949, when she departed Belfast for London to load for her maiden voyage. *Magdalena* left London for Buenos Aires on 9 March, but on arriving at the Argentinian coast in the early hours of 25 April, she ran aground on the Tijucas Rocks outside the harbour. Despite attempts to refloat her, she eventually broke her back and split into two sections; beyond effective repair she was declared a constructive total loss and thus became only the second vessel from Harland and Wolff to be lost on her maiden voyage as the result of an accident. Coincidentally, *Titanic* was also lost in the month of April some thirty-seven years previously.

Although such tragic events were keenly felt by everyone at Harland and Wolff, it could not be allowed to detract from the business in hand and the loss of *Magdalena* soon faded from importance. However, unbeknown to the workforce

Reina del Pacifico, Harland and Wolff ship number 852 and the scene of a tragedy in which many lives were lost.

another and more personal catastrophe waited just around the corner. The Pacific Steam Navigation Company's passenger liner *Reina del Pacifico*, built by Harland and Wolff in 1930, was undergoing a major refit after strenuous war service as a troopship. Work was completed by early September and the vessel left Belfast to conduct acceptance trials on the Clyde estuary, which were to include speed trials over the measured mile course off Ailsa Craig. All was proceeding as normal until the slight overheating of an engine cylinder was noted; without warning the engine exploded turning the engine room into a blazing inferno. In spite of the sterling efforts of the rescue party, the fires raged uncontrolled for several hours until eventually they were brought under control.

The scene that greeted the rescuers in the engine room was one of complete devastation: dead and dying men were lying everywhere suffering from severe burns and blast injuries. As the vessel was still technically undergoing repairs, the dead and injured were in the main Harland and Wolff staff, friends and colleagues of those who had battled so courageously to rescue them. The final death toll was twenty-eight, with a further twenty-three classed as critically injured and eighteen seriously injured. The shipyard manager in charge at the time, Alan Watt, was one of those most seriously hurt, receiving burns to over 60 per cent of his body and losing an eye. Coming so soon after the loss of *Magdalena*, the cataclysmic events on *Reina del Pacifico* had a demoralising effect on the workforce, many of whom had lost personal friends in the disaster. For several weeks an air of gloom and despondency hung over the shipyard as the funerals of those killed were held. Sir Fredrick Rebbeck attended every funeral and personally arranged for all those expenses that may not have been able to be met by the immediate family of the victims to be paid by Harland and Wolff. Despite his gruff exterior Rebbeck felt a personal affinity with his workforce. To him, Harland and Wolff was his family and in best Northern Ireland tradition a family always looked after its own.

After a relatively prosperous 1950, in which much of the groundwork done by Sir Frederick Rebbeck began to pay dividends, hopes were high that the coming year, designated as Festival of Britain year, would see the boom and bust cycle so prevalent in recent years finally laid to rest. The country was shaking off the last vestiges of wartime austerity: food and clothing rationing was almost over and an air of positivity pervaded the atmosphere. June 1951 gave every indication that Rebbeck was correct in his optimism as the order book stood at no less than sixty-eight vessels contracted; the oil tanker market was particularly buoyant with eleven firm orders on the books, the biggest being for a 32,000-ton oil tanker for British Petroleum, the largest such vessel to be built to date in the United Kingdom. A surprising but nonetheless welcome development was the upswing in Admiralty work after a break of almost seven years: Harland and Wolff received an order for two Whitby-class anti-submarine frigates, HMS *Torquay* and

Twin BP tankers outfitting at the wet basin.

Company transport in the 1950s.

HMS *Blackpool*. Since the end of the war tensions had continued to rise between the two great superpowers, the USA and the Soviet Union, which was enough to put the Admiralty on alert and anticipate that a number of specialised vessels might soon be required for the defence of the realm.

Apart from shipbuilding operations Harland and Wolff increasingly found itself in demand for standalone engineering tasks, which by November 1951 included fourteen electricity generator sets, three gas compressors and eight marine diesel engines for other shipyards. Much of this work was placed with the Finnieston works in an effort to increase the turnover of the facility.

Meanwhile, Queen's Island continued to enjoy an unprecedented level of peacetime activity: each slipway was occupied; the drawing offices were fully engaged in completing the design drawings for the next batch of orders; and the engine works had firm machinery orders stretching some three years into the future. Truly it could be said that the happy days were here again; nevertheless, as the old adage states, pride comes before a fall and just such a fall was about to hit the company.

Wednesday 31 January 1951 was just another normal working day at Harland and Wolff, and no one had any inkling of the terrible events that were to strike at the end of that day's shift. It had been a busy day completing outfitting of the 24,500-ton whale factory ship *Juan Peron* alongside the Thompson outfitting quay. Under normal circumstances the shift would finish with the manager in charge

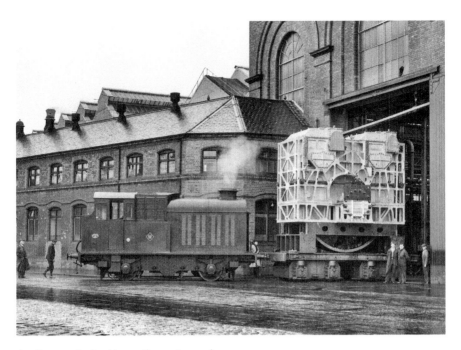

Another massive load leaves the engine works.

making sure the workers all assembled on the main deck of the vessel before permitting them to safely mount the gangway to the quayside. Unfortunately, due to illness the regular manager had gone home and the gangway was inadvertently left unattended, and more importantly uncontrolled. Anxious to go home at the end of a long and bitterly cold day, the workers crowded on to the gangway which, under the increased weight of so many bodies, suddenly collapsed, throwing several men into the water between the vessel and the quayside. The ensuing disaster consumed the lives of eighteen shipyard workers and badly injured another fifty-eight, thirty-two of whom were regarded as critical. The subsequent inquiry into the tragedy laid the blame squarely on a defect in the gangway construction which had caused it to collapse under the excessive weight of so many bodies. As a direct consequence of this calamity, Harland and Wolff introduced a self-regulating code of standards for all gangways in use at the shipyard to ensure such a tragic incident would never occur again.

During the summer of 1955 it became apparent that British shipbuilding was beginning to face stiff competition from foreign shipyards, in particular shipyards in Germany and Japan which had been substantially rebuilt after sustaining major damage during the war. As these yards were rebuilt they were able to install the most modern and efficient shipbuilding equipment and technology; the yards in the United Kingdom, by and large, had to make do with whatever they currently had available. As a consequence these foreign yards were able to quote startlingly

Juan Peron, Harland and Wolff ship number 1384, named after the Argentinian dictator.

Thompson Wharf outfitting quay, with Thompson dry dock to the right.

Southern Cross about to launch.

Southern Cross on sea trials.

low prices for new tonnage, in some cases less than the cost of the steel Harland and Wolff would need to build a similar vessel. Faced with such a dire set of circumstances, Sir Frederick saw no other option than to modernise Harland and Wolff up to and possibly beyond his foreign competitors. It was a simple matter of compete on a level footing or die and Rebbeck had no intention of going down without a fight.

Laying the first keel plate for *Canberra*.

Once again the sound of building work echoed across the slipways of Harland and Wolff, but this time it was more the sound of the concrete mixers than the clatter of steel upon steel. Rebbeck had been compelled to institute a programme of modernisation to the facilities. Many of the smaller slipways were amalgamated into much larger units, crane capacity was increased exponentially and underground mains services for gas, electricity and air were installed throughout the shipyard. So much building work was undertaken during this period that Rebbeck was humorously if irreverently given the title of Lord Cement; nevertheless, the improvements had the desired effect with the placement of the order by the Peninsular & Oriental Line in May 1957 for a new passenger liner to be named *Canberra*. With an initial contract price of £11,730,000, the order represented by far the most valuable ever negotiated by the company and at 45,270 tons, would be the largest liner to be built in the United Kingdom since the war. Unfortunately, this prestigious order was to prove something of an albatross around the neck of Harland and Wolff, as when the final tally of construction costs was added up, an eye-watering loss of £1,867,000 on the contract was revealed.

Sir Frederick Rebbeck took the news of this monstrous loss as a personal blow, however it had become clear for some time that Rebbeck was tired and showing the strain of having led the company for so many years. The Board recognised his momentous contribution to Harland and Wolff but at the same time accepted that he required much more support if he was to continue as chairman of the

The outfitting quay, with Thompson dry dock and the Queen's Shipyard in the background to the right.

company. To this end the Board recommended and pushed through a number of appointments, despite Rebbeck's insistence that he was fit and well. Dr Denis Rebbeck, Sir Frederick's son, was elected to the Board, not as many supposed at the time as a gesture to his father, but as an engineer of considerable ability in his own right; he even succeeded his father as chairman of the company in 1965. Further appointments included the promotion of J.S. Baillie as deputy chairman, who was given the specific remit to remove as much of the mundane work of chairman from Sir Fred as possible. For many years Baillie had played a significant role in negotiations with the various banks and had been instrumental in overseeing a much tighter financial regime within the company and the development of the business plan and strategy for the future.

Despite the changes to the Board, Sir Frederick continued to exercise almost autocratic control over the company and it wasn't until his eventual retirement in 1962 that his hand was finally removed from the tiller. Sir Fred epitomised Harland and Wolff; a man of steely determination and single-minded resolve, he lived and breathed Harland and Wolff almost to the point of obsession. During his years at the helm he had safely steered the company through some of the most dangerous times, and had rescued it from certain oblivion. His legacy and

P&O liner *Iberia* completing outfit at Victoria Wharf.

contribution stands proudly alongside that of Edward Harland, Gustav Wolff and Lord Pirrie as a doyen in the annals of shipbuilding, and Harland and Wolff in particular.

J.S. Baillie assumed the role of chairman on Rebbeck's retirement and continued to prove to be a safe pair of hands, strengthening many of the financial controls he had been instrumental in instituting. Although the order book remained in a healthy state, by the middle of 1965 the company's financial position was again beginning to give rise for concern. Overhead costs had spiralled almost out of control and, in the opinion of the Board, excessive amounts of overtime were being worked which only exacerbated the problem. Once again the Board found it necessary to make considerable changes to its structure, starting with the retirement of J.S. Baillie as chairman in 1965; he would be replaced by Dr Denis Rebbeck in the new joint role of chairman and managing director. Alan Watt, so badly injured in the *Reina del Pacifico* disaster, was appointed to assist Rebbeck as joint managing director, while R.S. (Ronnie) Punt took over directorship of the engine works.

The following year, 1966, opened on a note of uncertainty. The company again found itself on a downward track trapped in a web of unprofitable contracts which in turn damaged the cash-flow figures. A glimmer of hope came from an unexpected quarter when Aristotle Onassis, a major Greek ship owner and shareholder in Harland and Wolff, announced his interest in taking over the

Lifting a funnel by the floating crane.

Lowering a boiler into position.

company. The Board viewed this possibility with complete and utter horror, and Rebbeck was instructed to open a dialogue with the then prime minister of Northern Ireland, Terence O'Neill, to prevent just such an occurrence. Over a number of meetings between the two men Rebbeck succeeded in persuading O'Neill that the sale of Harland and Wolff to Onassis would be utter folly and would inevitably lead to the closure of the shipyard throwing several thousand mainly Unionist voters out of work. O'Neill, an Ulster Unionist, immediately saw the danger and agreed to do whatever he could to assist Rebbeck and the Board to thwart Onassis's ambitions.

The auditing firm of Price Waterhouse was instructed to investigate the financial position of Harland and Wolff and report to the Department of Finance for the government of Northern Ireland on the viability or otherwise of the government obtaining a controlling interest in the company. The report was completed on 28 June 1966 and presented to the then Minister of Commerce, Sir Brian Faulkner, who would later become prime minister of Northern Ireland. The report laid bare the financial position of Harland and Wolff and all but ruled out a complete takeover by the Northern Ireland government; however, this presented a dilemma, for Harland and Wolff could not be left to simply wither away on the vine – it had to be somehow made to function securely if it was

Typical working conditions in the 1960s.

to have a viable future. After months of protracted negotiation a compromise was reached which, as is usual in the course of such things, provided neither a satisfactory nor positive outcome.

Harland and Wolff, in return for a massive injection of public funds, would accept the need to be once again reorganised; particular emphasis was placed on the reconstitution of the existing Board, with government-appointed nominees to be given control of the company. It was a bitter pill to swallow but swallow it Rebbeck and his fellow directors did.

The first alteration to the Board structure was the appointment of a nominee from the Ministry of Commerce as financial controller and deputy chairman. Next, the Ministry was to vet and oversee all further appointments to the Board of Directors and, finally, John Mallabar would assume the role of chairman. John Mallabar was the senior partner of J.F. Mallabar and Company, a firm of chartered accountants based in the City of London. Mallabar also held various directorships in other companies and had been a member of the board of Plessey Electronics since 1946. Mallabar arrived at Harland and Wolff displaying all the bluster of a man in a hurry, yet with no particular affinity for Harland and Wolff or its history. He immediately set about slashing costs wherever he could and demanding that the workforce be considerably reduced with the simple, if probably flawed, reasoning

Victoria Wharf.

that a reduced workforce producing the same volume of output was by default working harder. Such a confrontational attitude was a recipe for disaster and, rather than increasing productivity, strikes and walkouts became the norm with the inevitable detrimental effect on production. Undeterred, Mallabar pressed on regardless, forcing through his policies against any opposition, eventually being rewarded for his efforts in 1969 by becoming Sir John Mallabar.

One of the changes Mallabar had demanded was the construction of a huge building dock surmounted with a gigantic overhead crane. For some time it had become apparent that vessels were growing in size so rapidly that conventional slipway launching was no longer practical or desirable due to the enormous strain this placed on the hull. The ideal location for just such a building dock was the Musgrave Channel outfitting area, a blind tributary of the River Lagan; its size and shape lent it perfectly for conversion to a building dock by simply damming the seaward end with a gate to create a gigantic cofferdam. Work commenced on the project in late 1967 which involved pumping out the water from the now-enclosed river channel and building a dam. The river banks were excavated and lined with concrete, while a large watertight gate was installed in place of the earth dam. By March 1970, although the dock was not fully complete, construction began on the first vessel at the new facility. *Esso Ulidia*, a 126,500-ton oil tanker for Esso Petroleum, was to be built in sections under cover and

Musgrave Channel, 1960.

Musgrave Channel before conversion to the building dock.

lifted into the building dock by the 1,000-ton lifting capacity, Krupp-Ardelt-built crane of Germany which was quickly christened Goliath.

Outwardly, things appeared to be progressing, but at the board meeting held on 11 March 1970 Sir John Mallabar castigated the failure of management to fully support his radical methods which had failed to stem the mounting losses. Faced with such an intransigent management he offered his resignation, citing that he had done all he could or was willing to do for Harland and Wolff. Needless to say, his resignation was gratefully accepted and the search began to find a replacement – hopefully a less controversial and belligerent one.

10

Stormy Seas in the 1970s

O nce again leaderless, the remaining Board of Harland and Wolff found itself in a strange quandary: the appointment of a new chairman and managing director would not be under their control. The government of Northern Ireland had harboured high hopes that by their appointment of Sir John Mallabar a step change in attitude would be effected within the company. Much to their disappointment this had not proved to be the case and from the confidential reports Mallabar had submitted to the Department of Commerce, such desired change seemed unattainable under the present management. Accordingly, the government had taken the decision that all future appointments to executive positions in Harland and Wolff would be at their discretion. This development was shattering news to the Board; not only were they being effectively neutered, but their powers to nominate successors had been completely removed. Events, however, were not allowed to drift and in June 1971 the Department of Commerce agreed a further financial aid package for the company, though it did not come without conditions. The new chairman was to be Lord Rochdale who had previously chaired the Committee of Inquiry into the shipping industry which was completed in May 1970 to much governmental acclaim, being both perceptive and far-reaching for the industry.

A new managing director was also to arrive, one who would have extensive knowledge and experience in the shipbuilding world and be a proven innovator. Rather surprisingly this nominee turned out to be Iver Hoppe, a Danish lawyer, who at the time of his appointment was also the managing director of a small Danish shipyard in Odense. Qualified as a lawyer, Hoppe had diversified into banking, eventually becoming chief executive of Den Danske Landmandsbank and a director of the Danish National Bank. Undoubtedly he was an extremely successful and intelligent man with a penetrating rationality and analytical judgement; however, whether this would be enough for him to rescue Harland and Wolff from its malaise remained to be seen.

The restructuring of the Board was completed with two further appointments: John Robinson, the former technical director of Shell International Marine and a member of the Shipbuilding Advisory Board, joined Christopher Gladstone,

Hornby Grange, a products tanker.

British Steel Corporation bulk ore carrier *Ravenscraig*.

a chartered accountant and partner in the accountancy firm of Schroder Wagg and Company. The final change to take place was the appointment of Douglas Cooper as financial director from his previous role as chief accountant. The new Board held its first complete meeting in August 1971 and was immediately faced with its first problem. An overtime ban by the steel-working trades had severely delayed production on a number of vessels, which in turn had detrimental consequences for the company's financial recovery.

The solution Hoppe devised was radical and innovative, yet devastatingly simple in its logic. Rather than be seen to be dictatorial, the Board would take the workforce into its confidence, explain its actions and by doing so enlist the workers' faith and support. Winning the hearts and minds of a demoralised and uncertain workforce would not be an easy task, but Hoppe was determined to try. His first action was to meet with the shop stewards to resolve their grievances and establish a more personal and hands-on relationship from the management side. Hoppe listened carefully to the criticisms and problems that had been allowed to fester for far too long and straight away resolved almost all of them, with the result that normal working was resumed by September. As a further gesture of his commitment to ensuring the workforce and Harland and Wolff had a positive outlook for the future, Hoppe resurrected a former plan to increase steel throughput to over 200,000 tons per year. The P200 programme, as it was known, had long since been abandoned as unrealistic and therefore unachievable under the current working practices; now with the support of the trade unions in accepting changes to established working methods and the relaxing of certain demarcation rules, both sides agreed that the programme goals could be realised.

Hoppe was delighted that his initial objectives had been so well received and on the union side the prospect of upwards of 5,000 extra jobs being created was nothing short of miraculous. Buoyed by his success, Hoppe approached Sir Brian Faulkner, the Minister of Commerce, for the additional funding the implementation of the programme would require. A study into the viability of the P200 programme had been undertaken by AB Svenska, a Swedish management consultancy who had estimated the cost of full implementation to be £20 million; however, this investment would be returned in increased production value over a period of fifteen years. The Department of Commerce was the one now on the horns of a dilemma: £20 million was a considerable sum of money to extract from the government purse, yet on the other hand the increased employment opportunities were attractive and could not be ignored. In addition, Northern Ireland was by this time experiencing ever-increasing levels of sectarian strife on its streets and the possibility of several thousand workers, mainly Protestant, being made unemployed did not bear thinking about.

The die was cast. The government of Northern Ireland simply couldn't afford *not* to support the P200 plan and therefore funding would be provided, but as usual it came with strings attached: 1) The company would receive no further governmental funding under any circumstances and must prove itself to be of commercial viability; 2) The government would accept no liability for any shortfall in the company's finances in the future; 3) The government would not under any circumstances seek to increase its shareholding in the company beyond the 47 per cent it currently held. It would, however, guarantee not to offer for sale any of its shareholding to ensure no takeover bid could be mounted for the company.

Confident now of the necessary support for the P200 programme, activity reached almost fever pitch on Queen's Island as the essential preparations were made. Behind the scenes, however, doubts were beginning to emerge at Stormont, the seat of the Northern Ireland government. Sir Brian Faulkner, now prime minister, had continued to view the increasing unrest on the streets with alarm. Many companies had seen a drastic downturn in business because of the troubles and the prime minister was increasingly aware that shipbuilding was one of the most vulnerable. Many ship owners had declined to bring their vessels to Belfast for repair due to concerns for the safety of their crews; to expect those same ship owners to base a technical team here for several months to oversee a new building was almost unthinkable. The social unrest spreading throughout Northern Ireland, together with increased competition from shipyards in the Far

Queen of Bermuda refit, April 1962.

Installing machinery on a passenger liner.

A prototype for a space helmet … actually a funnel cap for a Union Castle liner.

East – which had largely been rebuilt with American assistance after the Second World War – had made the position of Harland and Wolff look rather precarious and much rested on the shoulders of Iver Hoppe to deliver on his promises. Japanese shipyards with their modern equipment had a head start on European yards, which had not been re-equipped to the same degree; this, coupled with much lower labour costs, tilted the balance in favour of the Far East. Today, these same Japanese shipyards are facing almost the same situation as Harland and Wolff had faced, with the emergence of more cost-effective and modern shipyards in Korea, such as Samsung and Hyundai, and new shipyards in Vietnam.

Although rapid progress was being made to achieve the target for the P200 programme, Hoppe decided to recruit a specialist production manager to oversee the programme and to overcome any unforeseen problems. He found just such a candidate in Eric Hellstrom, a highly experienced technical manager from Kockums shipyard in Sweden. Hellstrom had spent his whole career with the Swedish shipbuilder and had ultimately been responsible for implementing the modernisation plan which had enabled Kockums to produce a completed ship hull, on average, every forty working days. So successful was Hellstrom in managing the P200 programme that six months after his arrival at Harland and Wolff he was appointed to the Board as technical director. At the same time, Ronnie Punt was made ship production director in place of Amos Sutcliffe, who had failed to meet expectations in that role.

Meanwhile, unrest continued to grow outside of Queen's Island with matters coming to a head when Brian Faulkner was summoned by the British prime minister, Edward Heath, to be bluntly informed that the UK government could no longer support the Northern Ireland government's position; therefore, the Parliament in Stormont must and would be dissolved with all legislative powers returned to Westminster. Faulkner was stunned at such a draconian state of affairs and bluntly refused to accept the announcement; his stance mattered little, however. The decision had been made and for the first time in almost seventy years Northern Ireland found itself without responsibility for its own affairs.

Despite such momentous developments, life continued much as normal at Harland and Wolff but the ramifications all too soon became apparent to the people on Queen's Island. The first of these was the imposition by the UK government of a wage freeze across the board at Harland and Wolff; this action caused particular rancour among the workforce because wages at the mainland shipyards had been allowed to rise above inflation levels.

Second was the restructuring of the British Steel Corporation which caused serious delays in the delivery of steel. In October alone over 10,000 tons was overdue for delivery to the shipyard, with the result that Harland and Wolff was faced with no other option than to turn to imports from Korea and Japan to maintain production and delivery dates for ordered vessels. Throughout the early 1970s, orders continued to be received at a trickle compared with a decade before. The orders may have been sparse in number, but the size of the vessels had increased greatly. Contracts were secured during the first half of 1973 for six 330,000-ton oil tankers and two 118,000-ton bulk carriers, which at least provided an optimistic outlook for the future. Outside the company the situation had deteriorated to a worrying level, with increasing time being lost through much of the workforce taking part in political demonstrations and protest strikes. The directors and senior management found the developing situation so serious that together with the support of the trade unions, they decided to reiterate their anti-sectarian policy, which stated that Harland and Wolff would be a neutral working environment for anyone in its employ. Subsequently, time lost to such activities was cut dramatically and Hoppe expressed his thanks publicly in the press to the trade unions for reducing sectarian tension within the shipyard and helping to maintain productivity at a high level.

Such had been the success of the Musgrave Channel/building dock development that the company now approached the Belfast Harbour Commissioners with the proposal to convert the newly opened Belfast Dry Dock ship repair facility into a building dock. The Harbour Commissioners were not receptive to this proposal, however, because they were already having trouble, due to the civil unrest, attracting enough ship repair work to maintain the facility. Such a frosty reception was mirrored in the industrial situation right

Three men in a boat checking *Queen of Bermuda*'s paint line.

We love work; we could
watch the man with the
broom for hours!

across the United Kingdom, with the winter of 1973/74 becoming known as
the 'winter of discontent'. Although Harland and Wolff was not overly affected
by this prolonged period of industrial unrest, the delays in receiving material
from the mainland did cause considerable dislocation to work at the shipyard.
Steel shortages were a particular headache which further halted progress on the
P200 target so important to Hoppe; rather than see employment increase under
this plan, the numbers had actually fallen due to a mixture of discontent and
disillusionment. Indicative of this sad situation was the departure of John Parker
in June 1974 to take up the position of managing director at Austin and Pickersgill
in Sunderland.

   T. John Parker had been an apprentice at Harland and Wolff and from his
earliest years with the company had demonstrated an incredible understanding
of the complexities of naval architecture and marine engineering. Training as a
draughtsman, he had rapidly gained a reputation as a gifted ship designer and
became the youngest ever head of the design department, bettering even the
achievements of the legendary Thomas Andrews. John Parker was a supreme
talent Harland and Wolff could ill afford to lose and the gap he left on his
departure would never be adequately or completely filled.

Productivity at Harland and Wolff continued to decline for the remainder of the 1970s, much to the displeasure of the new Labour government which had proven to be a much harder nut to crack in respect of financial support. The situation was not helped by the ever-increasing projection of losses and at the end of the decade, financial director Douglas Cooper presented Hoppe with the stark warning that by the end of June the company would be insolvent unless a direct government injection of capital was received. Hoppe relayed his concerns to the government together with an immediate plea for assistance, for which he received a curt response: 'The government will consider your request and respond by letter of its decision by 18 July.' Left in limbo by such an unsympathetic response, Hoppe departed for a planned business trip to Europe.

The government reaction came much quicker than anyone expected and was ruthless in its pronouncement: the government would take an immediate majority shareholding in the company; it would impose a strict level of pay restraint; it would take an executive position on the Board as opposed to the non-executive positions it had formally held; a new senior executive would be appointed by the government to oversee the position of the managing director, while also assuming responsibility for labour relations and pay. This was a shattering blow to the existing Board but, after a rather desultory discussion over lunch, the terms were despondently accepted.

Nevertheless, that was not the end of the matter. Upon his return from Europe Hoppe was summoned to the company's London offices for, he wrongly assumed, discussions on the new company structure. Upon arrival he was met by Alan Watt and Lord Rochdale who handed him a letter from the United Kingdom government advising him his services were no longer required and his resignation was effective immediately from today, 5 August 1974. Hoppe was stunned at such a brutal dismissal from his office and rather than return to Belfast, which he considered to be too painful to contemplate, he elected to go home to Denmark where shortly after his arrival he suffered a number of strokes from which he never recovered.

Things were equally gloomy on Queen's Island. The order for six massive oil tankers for the Maritime Fruit Carriers Company had been reduced to four, and then only two, and even these would result in a prolonged and expensive legal battle over delivery. The engine works was suffering from a complete lack of orders and was under consideration for mothballing or complete closure.

All was not lost, however, for the UK government had indicated it would continue to provide financial support for Harland and Wolff; but it was not willing to provide funds for what it considered to be speculative shipbuilding contracts. Any contract had to be with an identifiable ship owner who was acceptable to the Department of Commerce and could satisfactorily pass vetting checks as to his bona fides to qualify for ship mortgage facilities provided by the government.

The largest vessel built by Harland and Wolff: the 330,000-ton oil tanker *Coastal Corpus Christi*.

Shell 'L' class oil tanker *Lima* on sea trials.

The gloomy prospects behind the scenes were far removed from the public perception, which was of a shipyard producing record output. Indicative of this were three oil tankers for Shell Petroleum completed in 1976 which weighed 318,000 tons each – a combined deadweight of 954,000 tons. These vessels were, at the time, the largest ever built in the United Kingdom, only to be surpassed by the Maritime Fruit Carriers' oil tankers of 330,000 tons each. Productivity was up by an astonishing 45 per cent on the previous record set in 1974. A no less dramatic turn of events had occurred in the engine works, with orders being received for sixteen marine engines with a combined output of 275,000 horsepower and it appeared to all that Harland and Wolff was riding on the crest of a wave once more. However, all was not as rosy as it seemed, and may best be summed up by a comment made by Ronnie Punt: 'I would not like our figures to give the impression to anyone either inside or outside our industry that our troubles are over; we are far from it.'

That said, progress continued to be made for the remainder of the decade at, or slightly below, record levels. In contrast to this outward air of confidence, the 1980s opened on a rather disappointing note. A number of positive enquiries failed to develop into firm orders and the order book was empty, and had been that way since the last entry was made in November 1978. For fourteen months not a single order had been recorded – the longest lean period since the company began operations in 1861.

11

Death of a Giant: the '80s & '90s

T he beginning of 1980 saw the shipyard continue on a downward trajectory. Orders were not so much thin on the ground as non-existent and once again an enormous strain was placed on the company's finances. Reluctantly, the Board found themselves having to turn to the government for support. Something, or rather someone, would need to take firm hold of the tiller if Harland and Wolff were to emerge at all from the tempestuous waters it had been forced to sail. To further complicate an already difficult situation, British Shipbuilders Limited, the remaining and by now nationalised arm of the British shipbuilding industry, remained opposed to any further aid for Harland and Wolff, preferring to see what it considered its biggest rival disposed of as soon as possible. The relationship between the two diametrically opposed entities had been fractious ever since Harland and Wolff had avoided being nationalised as part of the British Shipbuilders consortium. Subsequent events had proven the wisdom of such a stance as many of the shipyards on the mainland had been ruthlessly closed by the government in a forlorn effort to reduce the strain on the public purse.

The now Conservative-controlled government had exercised a blunt logic towards shipbuilding in the United Kingdom; this crude and fundamentally flawed strategy was simply to withdraw UK yards from commercial shipbuilding altogether or leave the field clear for Harland and Wolff to capture any work it could on the global market. The remaining UK shipyards, such as Swan Hunter, Yarrow Shipbuilders and Vickers, would specialise in naval vessels only, primarily for the Royal Navy but would be allowed to export their designs or preferably accept orders from foreign navies. As any student of British shipbuilding in the 1980s will quickly realise, this overly simplistic plan was never going to work, the prime casualty being the venerable shipyard of Swan Hunter which, after struggling manfully against impossible odds, finally succumbed to inevitable closure due to lack of Admiralty work.

During this period John Parker had been appointed as deputy chief executive of British Shipbuilders Ltd and in that influential position had done much to repair the ill-tempered relationship between the two institutions; as an old Harland and

Wolff boy he still retained much affection for his old employer and doubtless felt Harland and Wolff would be better served under the British Shipbuilders umbrella rather than out in the proverbial cold. After much negotiation Harland and Wolff agreed to become a member company of the British Shipbuilding Research Association and agreed to collaborate with British Shipbuilders on future projects. A sign of the new relationship was the receipt of a much-needed order for the engine works from Govan Shipbuilders for two low-speed Burmeister & Wain engines. In addition to this most welcome order was the placement by Scott Lithgow of considerable design work with the drawing offices for an emergency support vessel for British Petroleum Shipping, eventually to be completed as *Iolair*.

Under the influence of John Parker an agreement was drawn up between the parties to allow Harland and Wolff to utilise the considerable marketing capabilities of British Shipbuilders to seek out orders for vessels beyond the latter's building resources. This era of co-operation heralded the prospect of a new beginning; one which Parker hoped would eventually see his beloved Harland and Wolff take its rightful place in the British Shipbuilders consortium and thereby open up shipbuilding opportunities currently denied to both organisations.

This dream proved to be rather over-optimistic, however, as the only orders taken in 1980 were for two oil tankers for British Petroleum, the other pair going to Swan Hunter who had shared the initial design and drawing production work with Harland and Wolff. Only two vessels were launched from the shipyard during this lean period, both were passenger ferries for British Railways: *St Christopher* and *St David*. The former was 'adopted' by the popular children's television programme *Blue Peter* and was officially launched by Miss Tina Heath, a presenter on the programme.

March 1982 saw the beginnings of an upturn once again in the merchant shipping market, leading to increased enquiries for new tonnage, in particular large bulk carriers. Harland and Wolff were actively pursuing several potential orders, the most encouraging of which was from a Norwegian shipping company, but at the eleventh hour this fell through because suitable financial guarantees could not be obtained from the UK government. Given that the order book was effectively empty once again and very little governmental assistance could be expected for securing further orders, the Board was faced with the unthinkable: the closure of the company. In an attempt to alleviate the fears of the workforce the Northern Ireland Office (NIO) stepped into the quagmire and attempted to assist by appointing another new chairman to replace Alec Cooke, who wished to step down as his interim appointment was coming to an end. Vivian Wadsworth was the choice of the NIO, chairman of Tank Investments, a large mining and finance group of companies; Wadsworth duly took up the reins of office in November 1982.

Regrettably, the strain of the previous tempestuous years began to take its toll on the long-serving directors; Ronnie Punt had had enough and decided to retire as soon as possible. Having been instrumental in the development of the VLCC

(Very Large Crude Carrier) design and having gone through the most wearisome and frustrating era in the company's history, his departure would be a mortal blow and he would be deeply missed for his energy and expertise. As a consequence of Ronnie Punt's retirement, the Board had lost what could only be considered as one of its most stalwart servants and a 'safe pair of hands'; soon the cracks began to appear in the structure. As a stopgap measure Douglas Cooper agreed to take over as managing director until a suitable candidate could be found to replace Punt.

The search for the new managing director proved an arduous and challenging exercise. Many candidates expressed their interest in the position but singularly failed to impress either the Board or the government, who had, as would be expected, taken a keen interest in who could provide the right combination of leadership, knowledge and business acumen. The answer was staring everyone in the face and in November 1982, to much elation, the news spread rapidly throughout Harland and Wolff. John Parker was coming back.

For those who had endured such a dark period in the company's history, the news that someone familiar and greatly respected had agreed to take up leadership of Harland and Wolff was the best possible Christmas present. His predecessor, Vivian Wadsworth, had done his best to keep the shipyard afloat but such a monumental undertaking had been beyond even his proven abilities and he was more than happy to relinquish control. A cliché it may be, but Parker knew his first task was to win the 'hearts and minds' of the UK government if he was to have any chance of succeeding where so many others had failed. From the government's point of view, Parker represented the last chance for Harland and Wolff; failure this time was simply not an option – Parker had to succeed in turning the fortunes of Harland and Wolff around. Being handed such a seemingly poisoned chalice did not outwardly bother John Parker; he knew the calibre of the workforce and the inherent pride they took in the job. He had an affinity with every one of them and now, having been given the opportunity to lead them, he was determined not to let them or himself down.

During his first week as chairman and managing director John Parker took the rather unusual step, although typical of his attitude and approachability, of personally touring each and every department in the shipyard and introducing himself to each and every employee. On many occasions, nevertheless, such introductions were unnecessary, as for many TJP, as he was known, was already a familiar and charismatic figure worthy of their trust. And so it proved to be, for within days of taking office Parker issued a directive to every employee, from first-year apprentice to director, that he did not wish to hear defeatist talk from any quarter: morale would be improved in all areas; he would make himself personally available to any employee with serious concerns; better communication from management would be a priority; and the best equipment and technological advances in shipbuilding would be obtained to enable Harland and Wolff to compete with the best shipyards in the world. His message did not go unheeded and morale underwent a significant improvement; the general feeling was that at last the company was going in the right direction with the right man at the helm.

Although future orders were proving hard to secure, measures were on-going throughout the shipyard to rationalise the facilities and introduce the new technology. The traditional drawing office was being adapted to embrace computer-aided design and the Steerbear design and draughting system was purchased from Kockums shipyard.

A state-of-the-art computer-controlled pipe bending and manufacturing shop was constructed on the site of the former boiler shop, and automated welding and cutting machinery was installed in the building sheds. Intensive negotiations took place with the trade unions to remove as much of the outmoded demarcation practices as possible, which gave rise to a fundamental change in the management structure. Gone was the traditional method of ship construction, whereby each trade performed its function and moved on; in its place came a 'zone'-based methodology where a section of the vessel under construction became the responsibility of an individual manager with a multi-qualified squad of tradesmen under his control. This method ensured the correct mix of skills was always available and they worked to complete their particular block of the vessel from basic construction of the shell to outfitting with the ancillary equipment etc. This 'zonal' method lent itself to producing much of the vessel under cover in the gigantic building sheds before transport to the building dock on specially designed transporter vehicles; it would then be lifted into place by the Goliath crane.

John Parker also looked abroad, chiefly to Japan, to obtain knowledge of other shipbuilding methods and practices to determine if such could be adapted to Harland and Wolff. It was exercises such as these that led to one veteran worker commenting: 'I've a bit of Krupp steel in my back from a German shell; I get a lift to work in an Italian car and now the ruddy Japanese are going to teach us about shipbuilding. If I had known all this in 1939 I would never have went to war.'

After protracted negotiations, British Petroleum, impressed with the commitment and expertise displayed by the Harland and Wolff technical team, decided to place an order for a revolutionary vessel with the company. The SWOPS (Single Well Oil Production System) was ground-breaking in its design and innovation; nothing like it had ever been produced before and such was the technological challenge in producing what was essentially a sea-going oil well and refinery, that even the government regulatory authorities for shipping had no idea how to classify such a unique vessel or indeed what construction standards to apply. The problem was eventually resolved with a composite classification: when sailing to the oil well it would be classed as an oil tanker; when over the oil well and either drilling or pumping oil it would be considered a production platform; and when storing the recovered oil it would be considered a storage installation. During this time an unusual and innovative contract was accepted from the Admiralty for an Aviation Training Ship (ATS), which involved taking a second-hand container ship, the *Contender Bezant*, and converting it into a mini-aircraft carrier, subsequently named RFA *Argus*.

Building on these notable successes, John Parker led the company into a new era in its history, positioned at the forefront of innovative and cutting-edge design. Over the past decade the Board had received an overhaul with many of the long-serving members opting for retirement, thus making way for younger talent better able to steer the company in its new direction. Among these changes was the departure of long-standing company secretary David Geary, to be replaced by the very experienced Trevor Neil. Douglas Cooper eventually retired from the Board in 1985 after being awarded a CBE in that year's New Year's Honours list, while in February 1985 William Gallagher returned to Harland and Wolff from British Shipbuilders as shipbuilding director. However, 1985 started on a note of great tragedy, for Kenneth Ruddock, the company sales director, developed a sudden illness and passed away on 24 January. Ken was a personal friend and contemporary of John Parker and had been an energetic and brilliant representative of the company. His warmth and engaging personality endeared him to almost everyone he came into contact with and his death was a deeply shattering blow to many who knew and respected him.

Harland and Wolff appeared to have turned the corner all over again and had largely reinvented itself by branching out into new and diverse fields. The way seemed settled for the future and the United Kingdom government saw the possibility of at last cutting its ties with the company. To this end a prospectus for its possible sale was prepared; a prospectus which would attract interest from an unexpected quarter and have major ramifications for the survival of the company.

12

Down But Not Quite Out … Yet

Morale and production had definitely shown noteworthy improvements since John Parker had taken control over the company, but its financial position remained on the critical list. Operating losses had increased year on year and the depletion of the balance sheet and working capital had proved impossible to correct. This most unsatisfactory situation was of particular concern to the Treasury who had up until now poured vast amounts of public money into a seemingly bottomless pit. Early in 1991 a decision had been made by a select group within the Treasury to divest itself of Harland and Wolff at the earliest opportunity; to forward this ambition the Treasury pressed for the appointment of Per Nielsen to the Board of the company. Nielsen was a Danish chartered accountant who had an established track record of disposing of loss-making shipyards in his native Denmark and wider Scandinavia. Duly appointed to the Board under the government 'golden share' arrangements, Nielsen replaced Douglas Cooper as financial director and deputy managing director.

As a partnership Parker and Nielsen were diametrically opposed in almost every regard: Parker was a shipbuilder through and through with a tremendous respect for the calibre of the workforce of Harland and Wolff and a deep regard for its history and industrial heritage. Nielsen, on the other hand, held no such affection for the company and regarded his position there in cold-blooded commercial terms. Given such a disparate combination, it was inevitable that a clash of personalities would occur. It was a situation Harland and Wolff most certainly did not need or want during the coming struggle for survival.

The posted losses for 1989 were a disappointing £2,890,000 on a turnover of just £6,770,000, despite every conceivable effort being made to address the continual haemorrhaging of cash from the company's coffers. Nielsen put in place draconian cost-cutting procedures across the board: all investment in or purchase of new equipment would be subject to his personal approval; a wage freeze was announced for all grades of staff; and a collection of austerity measures would be rolled out in all areas. Among these was the closure of the directors' dining room, known colloquially throughout Harland and Wolff as the Golden

All that remains today of the Queen's Shipyard.

Trough. This was accompanied by the closure of the management dining room, similarly known as the Silver Trough. In the future all grades of staff would use the communal dining rooms or canteens, but in practice very little integration was accomplished as the directors and senior staff almost universally chose to dine outside the company or make suitable alternative arrangements.

In the meantime, the Treasury had been busy working in conjunction with the government of Northern Ireland's Department of Commerce to find a buyer willing and able to remove Harland and Wolff from their responsibility. During the autumn of 1988 such a prospective buyer had been identified and a long series of protracted and highly secret negotiations were conducted in the main between the Treasury and the as-yet-unidentified potential purchaser. By Christmas of that year negotiations had progressed to such an advanced stage that both parties felt the time was right to reveal that talks had been taking place concerning the possible privatisation of Harland and Wolff in the near future. These revelations came as a complete shock to all but those at the highest level in the company, and gave rise to much disquiet and concern across the workforce. Memories of the attempted takeover by Aristotle Onassis came flooding back and the prospect was viewed by almost everyone with horror and anxiety. Amidst this atmosphere of apprehension the potential buyer was revealed as none other than Fred Olsen, the Norwegian shipping magnate, a figure almost unknown to the majority of the workforce in Harland and Wolff.

From that point events moved with astonishing haste for such a major transaction, and in February 1989 the announcement was made that Fred Olsen, under his two holding companies Atlan and Aztlan Shipping, had reached a provisional agreement with the United Kingdom government to purchase

The derelict Thompson dry dock pump house.

The former entrance to the Queen's Shipyard, birthplace of *Titanic*.

a controlling interest in Harland and Wolff. There were, however, a number of conditions to the successful completion of these arrangements, the principal ones being that the accumulated debt of Harland and Wolff, now standing at some £650 million, be wiped out in its entirety. All current and future liabilities of the company were to be assumed by the Department of Commerce, and the agreed total purchase price of the company and its assets was to be fixed at £12 million payable in instalments over five years, despite the company having a 'book value' of some £93 million. Finally, a golden hello of some £20 million was to be provided as a development grant to assist the new company in its transition from public to private ownership. Therefore, for the second time in its long existence, Harland and Wolff returned to the private sector after almost sixty years in whole or partial public ownership.

Concerned by the rather muted reaction to his purchase of the company, Fred Olsen embarked on what can only be described as a charm offensive towards a seemingly recalcitrant and singularly unimpressed workforce. Keen to do whatever he could to allay their fears for the future, Olsen promised that the workforce would have a major involvement in the running of the shipyard and by default their future would be in their own hands. Olsen sought to achieve this by giving all employees the opportunity to purchase shares in Harland and Wolff and by doing so take a personal ownership stake for the first time in what was essentially 'their' company.

Shares were priced at £1 per share with a suggested shareholding of 200 per manual worker or staff member, 500 for junior management, and a minimum of 1,000 for senior management or directors. To facilitate purchase of the shares a special loan arrangement was put in place so the share price could be paid in instalments, taken from salaries over an agreed period of time thereby negating any financial hardship. The share offering was an immediate success with around 97 per cent of staff; the 3 per cent unwilling to commit themselves to the company were regarded as pariahs and as such were deemed undesirable and subsequently dismissed. It must be said, in the interests of clarity and fairness, that there was absolutely no pressure on anyone to purchase shares or that share purchase was a guarantee of future employment.

The former Harland and Wolff Limited would pass into the ownership of the Northern Ireland Department of Commerce who would assume all its accrued liabilities, in particular the many thousand pending claims for asbestos damage to employees' lungs. The 'new' company would be known as Harland and Wolff plc for an interim period, until the final legalities of the employee buyout were finalised and other contract matters resolved. These issues were soon dealt with and by January 1995 the structure of the company had undergone a complete overhaul, culminating in the formation of several wholly owned but independently operating businesses. The largest of these was Harland and Wolff Shipbuilding and Heavy Industries Limited which was to undertake the traditional business of the original company. Complementing this was Harland and Wolff Power Limited, taking over the electrical works; Harland and Wolff Outfit Services Limited, responsible for the former joinery department; Harland and Wolff Technical Services Limited, the former design and drafting departments; Harland and Wolff Coatings Limited, the painting department; Harland and Wolff Ship Repair Limited, looking after the repair and general engineering business; and Harland and Wolff Properties Limited, which would look after the infrastructure and land assets of the group. All of these separate entities would

The main entrance to the Harland and Wolff complex; all these buildings are now demolished.

be controlled by the management organisation Harland and Wolff Holdings plc, reporting to the ultimate holding company Fred Olsen Energy S/A.

Each division had its own Board of Directors, yet in all cases at least one of these nominated directors was also a member of the Board of the controlling company. This unprecedented division of the various arms of Harland and Wolff created a number of senseless splits in the general group, and in the long run were abandoned as being unnecessarily divisive and from a practical standpoint completely unworkable. One example was the directive that the company medical facilities located within the shipbuilding company area would be unavailable to any other Harland and Wolff group employee. Such nonsense was rapidly disregarded, particularly as the medical staff fundamentally refused to deny treatment to *any* injured employee, irrespective of which division they were employed in.

Such petty and absurd directives became the norm, however, and only served to increase the sense of isolation many employees in the different subdivisions began to experience. Several of the smaller companies had by this time developed different working hours or holiday arrangements from the shipbuilding company, with the result that key staff necessary to support shipbuilding operations were absent at periods when their services were crucially required.

Inevitably, amid this mounting frustration a shattering blow was again to strike at the heart of the company. Although he had made every effort to return Harland and Wolff to its once envied position in world shipbuilding, circumstances precluded John Parker from achieving that worthy ambition. Increasingly exasperated and discouraged by the direction in which the company was heading, and seeing his strategy for the future hindered at almost every turn, he tendered his resignation with immediate effect and was replaced as chief executive by Per Nielsen.

Over the next decade the fortunes of the various Harland and Wolff group companies continued to decline. After just a year in existence Harland and Wolff Power was closed down, quickly followed by Harland and Wolff Coatings. The remaining subdivisions struggled on with their employment numbers suffering a slow but steady decline until the point of unviability was reached. In similar fashion the shipbuilding division also deteriorated, despite a clutch of orders being taken over the period. Two drill and oil exploration vessels were contracted by Global Maritime Corporation, the company once owned by the billionaire recluse Howard Hughes and famous for its construction of the *Glomar Explorer* vessel which attempted to raise a stricken Russian submarine from the ocean floor. These contracts proved an unmitigated disaster for the company, however, due to massive cost overruns which saw the contract price almost double, and a protracted legal battle to resolve the matter.

The final vessels to be built by Harland and Wolff were two general purpose roll-on roll-off transport vessels built for subcontract to the Royal Fleet Auxiliary service and managed by Andrew Weir and Company. The first of these was *Hartland Point*, entering service in late 2002, with the final vessel *Anvil Point* being delivered in 2003. With that poignant delivery and after almost 196 years, shipbuilding finally ceased on Queen's Island, and the tightly knit community that had grown up with and supported Harland and Wolff was devastated by the demise of the company.

Thompson dry dock abandoned and forlorn in the 1990s.

Livelihoods were lost at a stroke and thousands of men and women found themselves looking for alternative employment. The skilled professions so patiently learned over the years – such as shipwright, plater, caulker and loftsman – were not required outside the shipbuilding environment, of which Harland and Wolff was the only one in Belfast.

The social fabric of the area was torn apart with many families moving away in what was tantamount to a mass exodus of a once-settled community. With the death of their traditional source of employment, an air of depravation blighted the area, made worse by the many abandoned and derelict houses. Today, much redevelopment has taken place, which unfortunately has resulted in the loss of the evocative street names. The two massive Goliath cranes still dominate the skyline

Overgrown and neglected: Hamilton dry dock with a modern entertainment complex in the background.

The Harland and Wolff company logo.

over East Belfast as a poignant reminder of an industry unlike any other in the City of Belfast and a legacy of the greatest shipbuilding company in the world.

At the time of writing, Harland and Wolff still maintains a facility on Queen's Island; however, the company is largely unrecognisable from that which stood head and shoulders above all the world's great shipyards. Shipbuilding is unlikely to be undertaken again by today's Harland and Wolff, since the great shipbuilding sheds, the massive engine works, and all the machinery and infrastructure necessary for such an operation have long since been demolished or sold for scrap. The two giant cranes that dominate the Belfast skyline are now considered iconic images of the city, yet their colossal lifting ability is no longer required. Harland and Wolff continue to seek work in the offshore energy sector and have been successful in obtaining several contracts for the assembly of windmills to generate electrical power. In its heyday Harland and Wolff employed over 65,000 people directly in its operations and were responsible for a further 30,000 in subcontractors or material suppliers. The total today stands at only thirty-three permanent employees, with additional labour hired on short-term contracts as and when required.

The Queen's Island site itself is unrecognisable as a shipyard, the skyline now dominated by luxury apartment blocks, a hotel and assorted office blocks housing mainly financial and information technology companies. The latest addition has been the Titanic Signature Building, a £95 million development built on the site of the original slipway upon which RMS *Titanic* took shape. Whether or not such projects will herald a bright future for Queen's Island remains to be seen; certainly the spectre of Harland and Wolff prevails over the area and the ghosts of the many men who earned their livelihoods there still haunt the now-forgotten slipways. That the company survives today in one form or another is to be admired and the hope for its continued existence burns strong within the hearts of those surviving yard men for whom the memories of the glory days are still fresh and clear.

The history of Harland and Wolff, and in particular that of RMS *Titanic*, lives on in the Titanic Quarter development, which I originated, and the Titanic Signature Building on Queen's Island, which present to the general public a pictorial history of shipbuilding during what was perhaps the most innovative time in the industry. For several years I had struggled to get this concept accepted as a legacy of this great company and I am proud to look back on what has been achieved from the seeds I planted so many years ago. Recognised by Her Majesty Queen Elizabeth II by the award of the MBE for my work in preserving the maritime history of Harland and Wolff and *Titanic*, my greatest pleasure is to see the many hundreds of visitors to the former Queen's Island complex savouring and enjoying the sights and sounds of traditional shipbuilding at its very best.

13

Harland and Wolff Ship List

No.	Name	Type	Date Completed	Tonnage	Owner
1	Venetian	Cargo ship	14 August 1859	1,508	J. Bibby & Sons
2	Sicilian	Cargo ship	24 November 1859	1,492	J. Bibby & Sons
3	Syrian	Cargo ship	1 April 1860	1,492	J. Bibby & Sons
4	Cancelled				
5	Jane Porter	Sailing ship	15 September 1860	952	J.P. Corry & Co.
6	Miranda	Yacht	11 June 1860	34	Mr T. Yeats
7	Grecian	Cargo ship	30 January 1861	1,854	J. Bibby & Sons
8	Italian	Cargo ship	13 April 1861	1,859	J. Bibby & Sons
9	Egyptian	Cargo ship	11 August 1861	1,896	J. Bibby & Sons
10	Ballymurtagh	Hopper barge	4 September 1860	41	Wicklow Mining Company
11	Dalmatian	Cargo ship	21 December 1861	1,989	J. Bibby & Sons
12	Arabian	Cargo ship	2 May 1862	1,994	J. Bibby & Sons
13	Persian	Cargo ship	5 February 1863	2,137	J. Bibby & Sons
14	Castillian	Cargo ship	14 July 1862	607	J. Bibby & Sons
15	Catalonian	Cargo ship	2 August 1862	607	J. Bibby & Sons
16	Star of Erin	Sailing ship	31 October 1862	948	J.P. Corry & Co.
17	Recife	Sailing ship	24 November 1862	465	Mr James Napier
18	Worrall	Sailing ship	23 December 1862	484	Mr James Worrall
19	Alexandra	Sailing ship	8 June 1863	1,352	T. & J. Brocklebank
20	Star of Denmark	Sailing ship	21 June 1863	998	J.P. Corry & Co.
21	Victoria Nyanza	Sailing ship	15 August 1863	1,033	Joshua Prouse & Co.
22	Palestine	Sailing ship	11 October 1863	623	W.H. Tindall
23	Olano	Sailing ship	9 September 1863	445	Larrinaga Steamship Co.
24	Star of Scotia	Sailing ship	8 January 1864	999	J.P. Corry & Co.
25	Kitty of Coleraine	River boat	30 October 1863	24	Lower Bann Steamboat Co.
26	Waipara	Cargo ship	28 November 1863	90	J. Ritchie & Co.

No.	Name	Type	Date Completed	Tonnage	Owner
27	Baroda	Sailing ship	18 April 1864	1,364	T. & J. Brocklebank
28	Volador	Sailing ship	20 April 1864	174	G. Lomer
29	Star of Albion	Sailing ship	22 July 1864	999	J.P. Corry & Co.
30	Dharwar	Sailing ship	6 September 1864	1,456	Iron Ship Company
31	Douro	Cargo ship	21 November 1864	528	J. Bibby & Sons
32	British Peer	Sailing ship	11 February 1864	1,478	British Shipping Company
33	Sesostris	Cargo ship	9 May 1865	2,053	James Moss & Co.
34	Salamis	Barge	22 May 1865	64	James Moss & Co.
35	Sestris	Barge	14 June 1865	64	James Moss & Co.
36	Unnamed	Float	8 August 1865	102	Dublin Harbour Board
37	Pilot	Schooner	21 August 1865	158	G.W. Wolff
38	Fairy Queen	Paddle steamer	7 September 1865	149	Rock Ferry Co.
39	Gypsy Queen	Paddle steamer	8 September 1865	149	Rock Ferry Co.
40	Boyne	Sailing ship	21 September 1865	617	W.H. Tindall
41	Annie Sharp	Sailing ship	11 November 1865	584	R.G. Sharp
42	Duddon	Tug	9 November 1865	106	Hodbarrow Mining Co.
43	Guarani	Cargo ship	15 November 1865	320	J. Dalglish
44	Broughton	Sailing ship	3 January 1868	602	Ismay, Imrie & Co.
45	Candahar	Sailing ship	25 May 1866	1,418	T. & J. Brocklebank
46	Tenasserim	Sailing ship	18 September 1866	1,419	T. & J. Brocklebank
47	Istrian	Cargo ship	21 April 1867	2,930	J. Bibby & Sons
48	Iberian	Cargo ship	12 July 1867	2,930	J. Bibby & Sons
49	Illyrian	Cargo ship	25 September 1867	2,930	J. Bibby & Sons
50	Unnamed	Dock gate	5 July 1867	33	Belfast Harbour Commissioners
51	Black Diamond	Collier	8 July 1867	105	P. Evans & Co.
52	Camel Corsanegetto	Collier	16 August 1867	183	M.A. Corsanego
53	HMS Lynx	Gun Boat	19 June 1868	603	Admiralty
54	Hebe	Lighter	1 August 1868	157	W. & J. Phillips
55	Star of Persia	Sailing ship	10 June 1868	1,288	J.P. Corry & Co.
56	Woodlawn	Schooner	21 July 1868	63	S. Moreland
57	Star of Greece	Sailing ship	8 September 1868	1,288	J.P. Corry & Co.
58	Juliet	Sailing ship	16 January 1869	1,301	C.T. Bowring

No.	Name	Type	Date Completed	Tonnage	Owner
59	Elaine	Coaster	3 May 1869	544	F. Lervick & Co.
60–66	Unnamed	Harbour dredgers	4 May 1869	60	Dublin Harbour Board
67	Carry	Lighter	22 April 1869	81	W. Gossage & Co.
68	Bavarian	Cargo ship	5 November 1869	3,111	J. Bibby & Sons
69	Historian	Cargo ship	9 March 1870	1,830	T. & J. Harrison
70	Bulgarian	Cargo ship	20 March 1870	3,112	J. Bibby & Sons
71	Bohemian	Cargo ship	29 May 1870	3,114	J. Bibby & Sons
72	Unnamed	Floating dock	3 June 1870	107	Erne Waterways
73	Oceanic	Passenger ship	24 February 1871	3,808	Oceanic Steam Navigation Co. (OSNC)
74	Atlantic	Passenger ship	3 June 1871	3,708	OSNC
75	Baltic	Passenger ship	2 September 1871	3,708	OSNC
76	Republic	Passenger ship	21 January 1872	3,708	OSNC
77	Adriatic	Passenger ship	31 March 1872	3,868	OSNC
78	Camel	Cargo ship	17 September 1870	269	Harland and Wolff
79	Celtic	Passenger ship	17 October 1872	3,867	OSNC
80	Gaelic	Passenger ship	7 January 1873	2,651	OSNC
81	Belgic	Passenger ship	29 March 1873	2,651	OSNC
82	Star of Germany	Sailing ship	20 May 1872	1,337	J.P. Corry & Co.
83	Britannic	Passenger ship	6 June 1874	5,004	OSNC
84	Ferry No. 1	River ferry	1 October 1872	9	Belfast Harbour Commissioners
85	Germanic	Passenger ship	24 April 1875	5,008	OSNC
86	Star of Bengal	Sailing ship	7 March 1874	1,870	J.P. Corry & Co.
87	Belfast	Sailing ship	26 October 1874	1,957	T. & J. Brocklebank
88	Star of Russia	Sailing ship	12 February 1875	1,981	J.P. Corry & Co.
89	Majestic	Sailing ship	24 June 1875	1,974	T. & J. Brocklebank
90	Aglaia	Sailing ship	13 April 1875	821	Workman Bros
91	East Croft	Sailing ship	10 August 1875	1,367	W.J. Gambles
92	Connaught Ranger	Sailing ship	23 October 1875	1,200	J.G. McCormick
93	Millie	River boat	27 July 1875	107	W. Gossage & Sons
94	Katie	River boat	22 July 1875	107	W. Gossage & Sons
95	Fiji	Sailing ship	29 October 1875	1,436	W.J. Myers
96	Pizarro	Sailing ship	20 December 1875	1,439	W.J. Myers
97	Unnamed	Nile River barge	21 December 1875	114	W. Henderson & Co.

No.	Name	Type	Date Completed	Tonnage	Owner
98	Unnamed	Nile River barge	21 December 1875	114	W. Henderson & Co.
99	Unnamed	Nile River barge	22 December 1875	114	W. Henderson & Co.
100	Princess Beatrice	Paddle steamer	4 February 1876	556	Larne & Stranraer ferry company
101	Thursby	Cargo ship	16 July 1876	497	W. Thursby
102	Unnamed	Barge	3 June 1876	90	Cork Harbour Board
103	Lord Cairns	Sailing ship	25 January 1877	1,372	T. Doxon Hughes & Co.
104	Unnamed	Nile River barge	3 February 1877	114	W. Henderson & Co.
105	Mousmie	Yacht	14 November 1876	325	P. O'Connor
106	E.J. Harland	Sailing ship	1 June 1876	1,333	Thomas Dixon & Co.
107	Thurland Castle	Sailing ship	20 September 1876	1,301	Lancaster Shipowners Company
108	Steelfield	Sailing ship	1 January 1877	1,315	R.C. McNaughton & Co.
109	Gladys	Schooner	18 May 1876	52	N. Matheson
110	Slieve More	Jute clipper	24 March 1877	1,749	W.P. Sinclair & Co.
111	Slieve Bawn	Jute clipper	12 May 1877	1,749	W.P. Sinclair & Co.
112	The Lagan	Hopper barge	22 February 1876	55	A. Guinness & Sons
113	Star of Italy	Sailing ship	18 October 1877	1,644	J.P. Corry & Co.
114	Star of France	Sailing ship	5 January 1878	1,663	J.P. Corry & Co.
115	Slieve Roe	Sailing ship	16 March 1878	1,749	W.P. Sinclair & Co.
116	River Lagan	Sailing ship	14 August 1878	895	R. Neill & Sons
117	HMS Hecla	Depot ship	24 August 1878	3,360	Admiralty
118	British Empire	Passenger ship	10 August 1878	3,361	British Shipowners Ltd
119	Faugh-a-Ballagh	Barge	21 June 1878	500	Dublin Harbour Board
120	G.W. Wolff	Sailing ship	25 October 1878	1,663	S. Lawther & Co.
121	Nubia	Cargo ship	12 February 1879	1,958	African Steamship Co.
122	Shahjehan	Cargo ship	22 February 1879	1,650	Asiatic Steamship Co.
123	Shahzada	Cargo ship	14 April 1879	1,677	Asiatic Steamship Co.
124	Maharaja	Cargo ship	3 May 1879	1,666	Asiatic Steamship Co.

No.	Name	Type	Date Completed	Tonnage	Owner
125	Maharani	Cargo ship	5 June 1879	1,667	Asiatic Steamship Co.
126	Fair Head	Cargo ship	3 July 1879	1,175	Ulster Steamship Co.
127	British Crown	Passenger ship	8 October 1879	3,487	British Shipowners Ltd
128	Galgorm Castle	Cargo ship	21 August 1879	193	A. McMullan
129	Lord Dufferin	Sailing ship	14 November 1879	1,697	Thomas Dixon & Co.
130	Dawlpool	Sailing ship	24 January 1880	1,697	North Western Shipping Company
131	HMS Algerine	Gun boat	12 December 1880	835	Admiralty
132	Holmhurst	Cargo ship	12 December 1879	495	J.H. Thursley & Co.
133	Peshwa	Cargo ship	9 June 1880	2,159	Turner & Co.
134	Rosetta	Passenger ship	27 August 1880	3,457	P&O
135	White Head	Cargo ship	31 January 1880	1,192	Ulster Steamship Co.
136	Black Head	Cargo ship	14 March 1880	1,191	Ulster Steamship Co.
137	British Merchant	Sailing ship	7 October 1880	1,742	British Shipowners Ltd
138	British Queen	Passenger ship	15 January 1881	3,558	British Shipowners Ltd
139	British King	Passenger ship	29 March 1881	3,559	British Shipowners Ltd
140	Woodhopper	Barge	6 June 1880	47	OSNC
141	Arabic	Cargo ship	12 August 1881	4,368	OSNC
142	Coptic	Cargo ship	9 November 1881	4,488	OSNC
143	Minnehaha	Cargo ship	1 July 1881	1,390	Africa Steamship Co.
144	Akassa	Cargo ship	17 August 1881	1,389	Africa Steamship Co.
145	Shannon	Passenger ship	5 January 1882	4,139	P&O
146	Garfield	Sailing ship	19 February 1882	2,317	North Western Shipping Co.
147	British Prince	Passenger ship	4 April 1882	3,973	British Shipowners Ltd
148	Lord Downshire	Sailing ship	31 May 1882	2322	Thomas Dixon & Sons
149	Mandingo	Cargo ship	6 May 1882	1,700	Africa Steamship Co.
150	Walter H. Wilson	Sailing ship	18 August 1882	2,518	S. Lawther & Co.
151	Yucatan	Cargo ship	19 August 1882	2,816	West India Shipping Co.
152	Ionic	Cargo ship	28 March 1883	4,755	OSNC

No.	Name	Type	Date Completed	Tonnage	Owner
153	Doric	Passenger ship	4 July 1883	4,744	OSNC
154	British Princess	Passenger ship	19 April 1883	3,994	British Shipowners Ltd
155	W.J. Pirrie	Sailing ship	29 July 1883	2,576	S. Lawther & Co.
156	Fingal	Sailing ship	2 June 1883	2,570	R. Martin & Co.
157	Lord Woodley	Sailing ship	6 September 1883	2,576	Irish Shipowners Ltd
158	Dundela	Cargo ship	13 November 1883	876	Harland and Wolff
159	Dunluce	Cargo ship	3 November 1883	877	Harland and Wolff
160	La Nevera	Cargo ship	26 March 1884	359	River Plate Co.
161	Niger	Cargo ship	3 August 1883	2,006	Africa Steamship Co.
162	Dynamic	Ferry	13 December 1883	879	Belfast Steamship Co.
163	Guido	Cargo ship	12 January 1884	3,313	G.H. Fletcher
164	Bay of Panama	Sailing ship	12 January 1884	2,365	J. Bullock & Co.
165	Horn Head	Cargo ship	24 May 1884	2,496	Ulster Steamship Co.
166	Lord O'Neill	Cargo ship	12 July 1884	2,753	Irish Shipowners Ltd
167	Texan	Cargo ship	15 March 1884	3,257	West India Shipping Co.
168	Floridian	Cargo ship	16 August 1884	3,257	West India Shipping Co.
169	Benin	Cargo ship	24 July 1884	2,215	Africa Steamship Co.
170	Lord Lansdowne	Cargo ship	15 September 1884	2,752	Irish Shipowners Ltd
171	Belgic	Cargo ship	7 July 1885	4,212	OSNC
172	Gaelic	Cargo ship	18 July 1885	4,205	OSNC
173	Nurjahan	Cargo ship	27 September 1885	2,967	Asiatic Steamship Co.
174	Kohinur	Cargo ship	16 January 1885	2,967	Asiatic Steamship Co.
175	Callao	Sailing ship	26 January 1885	1,016	OSNC
176	Santiago	Sailing ship	4 March 1885	1,017	OSNC
177	Elbana	Barge	1 November 1885	347	Dublin Harbour Board
178	Teneriffe	Cargo ship	16 April 1885	1,799	British & Africa Steamship Co.
179	Elmina	Cargo ship	28 June 1885	1,764	African Steamship Co.
180	Costa Rican	Cargo ship	27 August 1885	3,251	West India Steam Navigation Co.
181	Irene	Ferry	29 September 1885	897	London & North Western Railway

No.	Name	Type	Date Completed	Tonnage	Owner
182	Zemindar	Sailing ship	14 August 1885	2,120	T. & J. Brocklebank
183	Talookdar	Sailing ship	24 September 1885	2,120	T. & J. Brocklebank
184	Queen's Island	Sailing ship	29 September 1885	2,093	S. Lawler
185	Iran	Cargo ship	16 March 1886	3,350	Edward Bates & Son
186	Saint Fillans	Cargo ship	24 September 1886	3,530	Rankin Gilmour & Co.
187	Caloric	Ferry	21 December 1885	942	Belfast Steamship Co.
188	Optic	Ferry	29 January 1886	880	Belfast Steamship Co.
189	Inishowen Head	Cargo ship	30 June 1886	3,050	Ulster Steamship Co.
190	HMS Lizard	Gun boat	4 February 1887	715	Admiralty
191	HMS Bramble	Gun boat	1 March 1887	715	Admiralty
192	Lord Templeton	Sailing ship	12 June 1886	2,151	Irish Shipowners Ltd
193	Ormiston	Cargo ship	30 October 1886	3,158	Irish Shipowners Ltd
194	Swanmore	Sailing ship	10 August 1886	1,821	W.J. Myers Ltd
195	Stanmore	Sailing ship	25 September 1886	1,824	W.J. Myers Ltd
196	Etolia	Cargo ship	9 April 1887	3,211	D. & C. MacIver
197	Minnesota	Cargo ship	22 November 1887	3,143	Torrey & Field Lyd
198	Lycia	Cargo ship	12 May 1888	3,223	D. & C. MacIver
199	Hercules	Dredger	8 March 1887	818	Londonderry Harbour Board
200	Michigan	Passenger ship	15 October 1887	4,979	White Diamond Steamship Co.
201	Oceania	Passenger ship	26 February 1888	6,362	P&O
202	Arcadia	Passenger ship	12 May 1888	6,362	P&O
203	Anglesey	Ferry	1 May 1888	887	London & North Western Railway
204	Sindia	Sailing ship	6 February 1888	3,067	T. & J. Brocklebank
205	Holkar	Sailing ship	30 April 1888	3,072	T. & J. Brocklebank
206	Idar	Cargo ship	3 July 1888	4,049	F. Leyland & Co.
207	Bostonian	Cargo ship	11 August 1888	4,472	OSNC
208	Teutonic	Passenger ship	25 July 1888	9,685	OSNC
209	Majestic	Passenger ship	22 March 1890	9,861	OSNC
210	Cufic	Livestock carrier	1 December 1888	4,639	OSNC
211	Runic	Livestock carrier	16 February 1889	4,639	OSNC
212	Palmas	Cargo ship	13 October 1888	2,428	Sir A.L. Jones

No.	Name	Type	Date Completed	Tonnage	Owner
213	Lord Londonderry	Cargo ship	6 December 1888	2,409	Irish Shipowners Ltd
214	British Empire	Cargo ship	13 April 1889	3,020	British Shipowners Ltd
215	Queensmore	Cargo ship	26 July 1889	4,195	William Johnstone
216	Lancashire	Cargo ship	10 August 1889	3,870	Bibby Steamship Co.
217	Yorkshire	Cargo ship	5 October 1889	3,870	Bibby Steamship Co.
218	Ameer	Cargo ship	17 October 1889	4,014	T. & J. Brocklebank
219	Gaekwar	Cargo ship	15 March 1890	4,202	T. & J. Brocklebank
220	Nawab	Cargo ship	23 November 1889	3,142	Asiatic Steamship Co.
221	Nadir	Cargo ship	24 December 1889	3,142	Asiatic Steamship Co.
222	Nizam	Cargo ship	26 February 1890	3,142	Asiatic Steamship Co.
223	Alexander Elder	Cargo ship	19 April 1890	4,173	Elder Dempster
224	Saint Pancras	Cargo ship	13 May 1890	4,283	Rankin Gilmour & Co.
225	California	Sailing ship	24 April 1890	3,099	North Western Shipping
226	Imaum	Cargo ship	31 May 1890	4,129	Edward Bates & Son
227	Michigan	Cargo ship	21 June 1890	3,722	Baltimore Lighterage Co.
228	Plassey	Cargo ship	5 July 1890	3,175	T. & J. Brocklebank
229	Columbian	Cargo ship	23 August 1890	5,088	F. Leyland & Co.
230	Georgian	Cargo ship	27 September 1890	5,088	F. Leyland & Co.
231	Mississippi	Cargo ship	18 October 1890	3,731	Baltimore Lighterage Co.
232	Sobranon	Cargo ship	6 November 1890	3,185	African Steamship Co.
233	Memphis	Cargo ship	27 November 1890	3,190	Elder Dempster
234	Ernesto	Cargo ship	11 December 1890	2,573	G.H. Fletcher & Co.
235	British Crown	Passenger ship	17 January 1891	3,205	British Shipowners Ltd
236	Nomadic	Livestock carrier	14 April 1891	5,749	OSNC
237	Tauric	Livestock carrier	16 May 1891	5,727	OSNC
238	Labrador	Passenger ship	13 August 1891	4,737	Dominion Steamship Co.
239	Assaye	Cargo ship	4 July 1891	4,296	Elder Dempster
240	Cheshire	Passenger ship	3 September 1891	5,656	Bibby Steamship Co.

No.	Name	Type	Date Completed	Tonnage	Owner
241	Shropshire	Passenger ship	3 October 1891	5,660	Bibby Steamship Co.
242	Ionia	Cargo ship	12 January 1892	6,335	D. & C. MacIver
243	Lancastrian	Cargo ship	17 October 1891	5,120	F. Leyland & Co.
244	Philadelphian	Cargo ship	12 November 1891	5,120	F. Leyland & Co.
245	Pindari	Cargo ship	5 December 1891	5,674	T. & J. Brocklebank
246	Mahratta	Cargo ship	28 January 1892	5,680	T. & J. Brocklebank
247	Massachusetts	Passenger ship	5 March 1892	5,590	Baltimore Lighterage Co.
248	Manitoba	Passenger ship	9 April 1892	5,591	Baltimore Lighterage Co.
249	Mohawk	Passenger ship	7 May 1892	5,575	Elder Dempster
250	Lord Erne	Cargo ship	28 May 1892	5,828	Irish Shipowners Ltd
251	Naronic	Livestock carrier	11 July 1892	6,594	OSNC
252	Bovic	Livestock carrier	22 August 1892	6,583	OSNC
253	Mobile	Cargo ship	27 July 1892	5,779	African Steamship Co.
254	Nurani	Cargo ship	10 September 1892	4,432	Asiatic Steamship Co.
255	Nairung	Cargo ship	10 November 1892	4,425	Asiatic Steamship Co.
256	Sagamore	Passenger ship	30 November 1892	5,036	Geo Warren & Co.
257	Islam	Cargo ship	15 December 1892	5,404	Edward Bates & Son
258	Damson Hill	Sailing ship	18 January 1893	2,087	W.J. Myers & Co.
259	Orellana	Passenger ship	23 February 1893	4,822	Pacific Steam Navigation Company (PSNC)
260	Antisana	Cargo ship	11 March 1893	3,584	PSNC
261	Gaul	Passenger ship	6 May 1893	4,754	Union Steamship Co.
262	Lord Templemore	Sailing ship	19 April 1892	3,054	Irish Shipowners Ltd
263	Goth	Passenger ship	8 June 1893	4,738	Union Steamship Co.
264	Orcana	Passenger ship	8 July 1893	4,821	PSNC
265	Sarmiento	Passenger ship	17 June 1893	3,606	PSNC
266	Mystic	Ferry	1 April 1893	726	Belfast Steamship Co.
267	Gothic	Passenger ship	28 November 1893	7,667	OSNC
268	Greek	Passenger ship	26 August 1893	4,744	Union Steamship Co.
269	Magnetic	Passenger tender	6 June 1891	619	OSNC

No.	Name	Type	Date Completed	Tonnage	Owner
270	Cevic	Livestock carrier	6 January 1894	8,301	OSNC
271	Magic	Ferry	10 August 1893	1,630	Belfast Steamship Co.
272	Sachem	Passenger ship	28 October 1893	5,203	Geo Warren & Co.
273	Magellan	Cargo ship	23 November 1893	5,910	PSNC
274	Torr Head	Cargo ship	7 April 1894	3,593	Ulster Steamship Co.
275	Inca	Cargo ship	28 December 1893	3,593	PSNC
276	Unnamed	Dredger	11 May 1893	60	Lower Bann River Trust
277	Templemore	Cargo ship	7 February 1894	6,276	William Johnstone
278	Staffordshire	Passenger ship	2 April 1894	6,005	Bibby Steamship Co.
279	Ikbal	Cargo ship	5 May 1894	5,404	Edward Bates & Son
280	Norman	Passenger ship	13 October 1894	7,392	Union Steamship Co.
281	Prussia	Passenger ship	31 May 1894	5,840	Hamburg Amerika Line
282	Persia	Passenger ship	15 July 1894	5,857	Hamburg Amerika Line
283	Pontic	Baggage tender	13 April 1894	395	OSNC
284	Guelph	Passenger ship	8 September 1894	4,917	Union Steamship Co.
285	Oropesa	Passenger ship	9 February 1895	5,317	PSNC
286	Orissa	Passenger ship	30 March 1895	5,317	PSNC
287	Blairmore	Cargo ship	17 October 1894	2,286	William Johnstone
288	Ulstermore	Cargo ship	6 December 1894	6,326	William Johnstone
289	Scotsman	Passenger ship	11 April 1895	6,041	Richard Mills & Co.
290	Marino	Cargo ship	2 March 1895	5,819	Thomas Dixon & Sons
291	Victorian	Passenger ship	31 August 1895	8,767	F. Leyland & Co.
292	Armenian	Passenger ship	19 September 1895	8,765	F. Leyland & Co.
293	Georgic	Livestock carrier	8 August 1895	10,077	OSNC
294	American	Cargo ship	8 October 1895	8,196	West India & Pacific Steam Navigation Co.
295	Historian	Cargo ship	29 January 1896	6,857	Charente Steamship Co.
296	Cestrian	Passenger ship	5 March 1896	8,761	F. Leyland & Co.
297	Iran	Cargo ship	30 April 1896	6,250	Edward Bates & Son
298	Vedamore	Cargo ship	28 March 1896	6,329	William Johnstone
299	China	Passenger ship	28 November 1896	7,899	P&O

No.	Name	Type	Date Completed	Tonnage	Owner
300	Canada	Passenger ship	26 September 1896	8,800	Dominion Line
301	Istrar	Cargo ship	4 June 1896	4,584	Edward Bates & Son
302	Pennsylvania	Passenger ship	30 January 1897	13,726	Hamburg Amerika Line
303	European	Cargo ship	3 December 1896	8,194	West India & Pacific Steam Navigation Co.
304	Gascon	Passenger ship	13 February 1897	6,288	Union Steamship Line
305	Gaika	Passenger ship	15 April 1897	6,287	Union Steamship Line
306	Comic	Ferry	25 September 1896	903	Belfast Steamship Co.
307	Arabia	Cargo ship	7 March 1897	5,550	Hamburg Amerika Line
308	Arcadia	Cargo ship	2 April 1897	5,551	Hamburg Amerika Line
309	Delphic	Passenger ship	15 May 1897	8,273	OSNC
310	Oravia	Passenger ship	12 June 1897	5,320	PSNC
311	Goorkha	Passenger ship	28 August 1897	6,286	Union Steamship Co.
312	Rotterdam	Passenger ship	29 July 1897	8,301	Holland-America Line
313	Briton	Passenger ship	26 November 1897	10,248	Union Steamship Line
314	Derbyshire	Passenger ship	8 October 1897	6,635	Bibby Steamship Co.
315	New England	Passenger ship	30 June 1898	11,394	Richard Mills & Co.
316	Cymric	Passenger ship	5 February 1898	12,551	OSNC
317	Oceanic	Passenger ship	26 August 1899	17,274	OSNC
318	Brasilia	Passenger ship	21 March 1898	10,961	Hamburg Amerika Line
319	Winifreda	Passenger ship	17 February 1898	6,833	F. Leyland & Co.
320	Statendam	Passenger ship	18 August 1898	10,319	Holland-America Line
321	Bay State	Cargo ship	31 August 1898	6,824	Goerge Warren & Co.
322	Afric	Passenger ship	2 February 1899	11,984	OSNC
323	Medic	Passenger ship	6 July 1899	11,985	OSNC
324	Winifredan	Passenger ship	8 July 1899	10,404	F. Leyland & Co.
325	Persic	Passenger ship	16 November 1899	11,973	OSNC
326	Saxon	Passenger ship	9 June 1900	12,385	Union Steamship Co.
327	Michigan	Passenger ship	14 December 1899	9,494	Atlantic Transport Co.

No.	Name	Type	Date Completed	Tonnage	Owner
328	Minneapolis	Passenger ship	29 March 1900	13,401	Atlantic Transport Co.
329	Minnehaha	Passenger ship	7 July 1900	13,714	Atlantic Transport Co.
330	Commonwealth	Passenger ship	22 September 1900	12,096	Richard Mills & Co.
331	Devonian	Passenger ship	6 September 1900	10,417	F. Leyland & Co.
332	Runic	Passenger ship	22 December 1900	12,482	OSNC
333	Suevic	Passenger ship	9 March 1901	12,531	OSNC
334	German	Passenger ship	10 November 1898	6,763	Union Steamship Co.
335	Celtic	Passenger ship	11 July 1901	20,904	OSNC
336	Ryndam	Passenger ship	3 October 1901	12,302	Holland-America Line
337	Cedric	Passenger ship	31 January 1903	21,073	OSNC
338	Noordam	Passenger ship	29 March 1902	12,316	Holland-America Line
339	Minnetonka	Passenger ship	17 May 1902	13,397	Atlantic Transport Co.
340	Arabic	Passenger ship	21 June 1903	15,801	OSNC
341	Athenic	Passenger ship	23 January 1902	12,234	OSNC
342	Walmer Castle	Passenger ship	20 February 1902	12,545	Union Castle
343	Corinthic	Passenger ship	14 July 1902	12,231	OSNC
344	Warwickshire	Passenger ship	6 March 1902	7,966	Bibby Steamship Co.
345	Columbus	Passenger ship	12 September 1903	15,378	Richard Mills & Co.
346	Ionic	Passenger ship	15 December 1902	12,232	OSNC
347	Galeka	Passenger ship	23 December 1899	6,767	Union Steamship Co.
348	Galician	Passenger ship	6 December 1900	6,756	Union Steamship Co.
349	Iowa	Passenger ship	11 November 1902	8,369	George Warren & Co.
350	Marmora	Passenger ship	19 November 1903	10,522	P&O
351	Orita	Passenger ship	26 March 1903	9,230	PSNC
352	Baltic	Passenger ship	23 June 1904	23,875	OSNC
353	President Lincoln	Passenger ship	14 May 1907	18,073	Hamburg Amerika Line
354	President Grant	Passenger ship	3 September 1907	18,089	Hamburg Amerika Line
355	Macedonia	Passenger ship	28 January 1904	10,511	P&O
356	Kenilworth Castle	Passenger ship	14 May 1904	12,975	Union Castle
357	Amerika	Passenger ship	21 September 1905	22,724	Hamburg Amerika Line
358	Adriatic	Passenger ship	25 April 1907	24,540	OSNC

No.	Name	Type	Date Completed	Tonnage	Owner
359	Worcestershire	Passenger ship	17 September 1904	7,160	Bibby Steamship Co.
360	HMS Enchantress	Yacht	11 June 1904	2,514	Admiralty
361	Dunluce Castle	Passenger ship	15 September 1904	8,133	Union Castle
362	Slievemore	Ferry	17 October 1904	1,138	London & North Western Railway
363	Pardo	Cargo ship	1 October 1904	4,365	Royal Mail Line
364	Potaro	Cargo ship	8 December 1904	4,378	Royal Mail Line
365	Mamari	Passenger ship	3 December 1904	6,689	Shaw Savill & Albion Co.
366	Nieuw Amsterdam	Passenger ship	22 February 1906	16,913	Holland-America Line
367	Aragon	Passenger ship	22 June 1905	9,441	Royal Mail
368	Bologna	Cargo ship	25 May 1905	4,603	Hamburg Amerika Line
369	Maharonda	Cargo ship	3 August 1905	7,630	T. & J. Brocklebank
370	Slieve Bawn	Ferry	10 October 1905	1,147	London & North Western Railway
371	Herefordshire	Passenger ship	29 November 1905	7,183	Bibby Steamship Co.
372	Amazon	Passenger ship	5 June 1906	10,036	Royal Mail
373	Malakand	Cargo ship	14 December 1906	7,653	T. & J. Brocklebank
374	Manipur	Cargo ship	13 January 1906	7,564	T. & J. Brocklebank
375	Matheran	Cargo ship	12 May 1906	7,653	T. & J. Brocklebank
376	Ortega	Cargo ship	28 June 1906	7,970	PSNC
377	Oronsa	Cargo ship	16 August 1906	7,907	PSNC
378	Heroic	Ferry	23 April 1906	2,016	Belfast Steamship Co.
379	Graphic	Ferry	19 May 1906	2,016	Belfast Steamship Co.
380	Salamanca	Cargo ship	15 September 1906	5,969	Hamburg Amerika Line
381	Rohilla	Cargo ship	17 November 1906	7,413	British India Steam Navigation Co.
382	Avon	Passenger ship	15 June 1907	11,072	Royal Mail
383	Aburi	Cargo ship	2 January 1907	3,730	Elder Dempster
384	Sierra Leone	Cargo ship	8 January 1907	3,730	Elder Dempster
385	Iroquois	Oil tanker	19 October 1907	9,201	Anglo American Oil Co.
386	Fulani	Cargo ship	1 June 1907	3,730	Elder Dempster
387	Prashu	Cargo ship	29 June 1907	3,755	Elder Dempster
388	Asturias	Passenger ship	8 January 1908	12,001	Royal Mail

No.	Name	Type	Date Completed	Tonnage	Owner
389	Navahoe	Oil barge	18 January 1908	390	Anglo American Oil Company
390	Rotterdam	Passenger ship	3 June 1908	23,980	Holland-America Line
391	Belgic	Passenger ship	21 June 1917	24,147	International Navigation Co.
392	Pericles	Passenger ship	4 June 1908	10,924	George Thompson & Co.
393	Lapland	Passenger ship	27 March 1909	18,565	Red Star Line
394	Laurentic	Passenger ship	15 April 1909	14,892	OSNC
395	Median	Cargo ship	25 January 1908	6,296	F. Leyland & Co.
396	Memphian	Cargo ship	20 February 1908	6,305	F. Leyland & Co.
397	Minnewaska	Passenger ship	24 April 1909	14,816	Atlantic Transport Co.
398	Mercian	Cargo ship	16 May 1908	6,304	Furness Leyland Line
399	Megantic	Passenger ship	3 June 1909	14,877	OSNC
400	Olympic	Passenger ship	31 May 1911	45,324	OSNC
401	Titanic	Passenger ship	2 April 1912	46,328	OSNC
402	Leopoldville	Passenger ship	10 November 1908	5,350	Compagnie Belge Maritime du Congo
403	Leicestershire	Passenger ship	11 September 1909	8,339	Bibby Steamship Co.
404	Karoola	Passenger ship	8 July 1909	7,390	McIlwraith & McEachearn Ltd
405	Berbice	Cargo ship	8 July 1909	2,379	Royal Mail
406	Balantia	Cargo ship	18 December 1909	2,379	Royal mail
407	Mallina	Cargo ship	29 April 1909	3,213	Australasian Steam Navigation Co.
408	Meltonian	Cargo ship	17 August 1909	6,306	Furness Leyland Line
409	Pakeha	Cargo ship	20 August 1909	7,910	Shaw Savill
410	Edinburgh Castle	Passenger ship	28 April 1910	13,326	Union Castle
411	Gloucestershire	Passenger ship	22 October 1910	8,334	Bibby Steamship Co.
412	Themistocles	Passenger ship	12 January 1911	11,213	George Thompson & Co.
413	Sachen	Passenger ship	21 January 1911	7,966	Hamburg Amerika Line
414	Maloja	Passenger ship	7 September 1911	12,430	P&O
415	Arlanza	Passenger ship	8 June 1912	15,043	Royal Mail
416	Bayern	Passenger ship	16 February 1911	7,986	Hamburg Amerika Line
417	Preussen	Passenger ship	13 December 1910	7,986	Hamburg Amerika Line

No.	Name	Type	Date Completed	Tonnage	Owner
418	Demosthenes	Passenger ship	5 August 1911	11,223	George Thompson & Co.
419	Galway Castle	Passenger ship	9 October 1911	7,987	Union Castle
420	Deseado	Passenger ship	27 June 1912	11,471	Royal Mail
421	Zealandic	Passenger ship	12 October 1911	10,879	OSNC
422	Nomadic	Passenger tender	27 May 1911	1,260	OSNC
423	Traffic	Passenger tender	27 May 1911	639	OSNC
424	Patriotic	Ferry	28 March 1912	2,254	Belfast Steamship Co.
425	Demerara	Passenger ship	8 August 1912	11,484	Royal Mail
426	Desna	Passenger ship	3 October 1912	11,483	Royal Mail
427	Darro	Passenger ship	31 October 1912	11,484	Royal Mail
428	Drina	Passenger ship	16 January 1913	11,484	Royal Mail
429	Oxfordshire	Passenger ship	17 September 1912	8,623	Bibby Steamship Co.
430	Abosso	Cargo ship	19 December 1912	7,782	Africa Steamship Co.
431	Appam	Passenger ship	27 February 1913	7,781	British & African Steamship Co.
432	Ceramic	Passenger ship	5 July 1913	18,481	OSNC
433	Britannic	Passenger ship	8 December 1915	48,158	OSNC
434	Andes	Passenger ship	12 September 1913	15,620	PSNC
435	Alcantara	Passenger ship	28 May 1914	15,831	Royal Mail
436	Justicia	Passenger ship	7 April 1917	32,234	OSNC
437	Katoomba	Passenger ship	10 July 1913	9,424	McIlwraith & McEachern & Co.
438	Orduna	Passenger ship	22 January 1914	15,499	PSNC
439	Euripides	Passenger ship	6 June 1914	14,947	George Thompson & Co.
440	Orbita	Passenger ship	31 July 1915	15,678	PSNC
441	Almanzora	Passenger ship	7 October 1915	16,034	Royal Mail
442	Orca	Passenger ship	25 May 1918	15,120	PSNC
443	Apapa	Passenger ship	4 March 1915	7,832	Elder Dempster
444	Egba	Cargo ship	5 April 1914	4,989	Elder Dempster
445	Egori	Cargo ship	21 June 1914	4,995	Elder Dempster
446	Minnekahda	Passenger ship	21 March 1918	17,220	Atlantic Transport Co.
447	Attendant	Passenger tender	21 August 1913	317	Elder Dempster
448	Maryland	Passenger ship	1 November 1913	4,731	Atlantic Transport Co.
449	Missouri	Passenger ship	28 February 1914	4,707	Atlantic Transport Co.
450	Mississippi	Passenger ship	5 November 1914	4,717	Atlantic Transport Co.

No.	Name	Type	Date Completed	Tonnage	Owner
451	Falistra	Cargo ship	31 March 1915	4,344	East Asiatic Company
452	Kangaroo	Cargo ship	22 October 1915	4,384	Western Australian Government
453	Brecknockshire	Cargo ship	11 January 1917	8,422	Royal Mail
454	Regina	Passenger ship	26 October 1918	16,313	Dominion Line
455	Arundel Castle	Passenger ship	8 April 1921	19,500	Union Castle
456	Windsor Castle	Passenger ship	11 March 1922	19,022	Union Castle
457	Pittsburg	Passenger ship	25 May 1922	16,322	American Line
458	Rimouski	Cargo ship	11 July 1918	9,281	Dominion Line
459	Lancashire	Passenger ship	9 August 1917	9,445	Bibby Steamship Co.
460	Millais	Cargo ship	18 September 1917	7,300	Lamport & Holt
461	Vedic	Cargo ship	10 July 1918	9,332	OSNC
462	Marconi	Cargo ship	1 February 1917	7,402	Lamport & Holt
463	Melita	Passenger ship	12 January 1918	13,967	Canadian Pacific Railways
464	Minnedosa	Passenger ship	21 November 1918	13,972	Canadian Pacific Railways
465	Glenavy	Cargo ship	1 September 1917	5,975	Glen Line
466	Glengyle	Cargo ship	7 December 1915	6,225	Glen Line
467	Glenartney	Cargo ship	16 May 1916	7,273	Glen Line
468	Glenamoy	Cargo ship	22 September 1916	7,269	Glen Line
469	Nederland	Passenger ship	Abandoned on slipway	26,500	Red Star Line
470	Laurentic	Passenger ship	1 November 1927	18,724	OSNC
471	Narkunda	Passenger ship	30 March 1920	16,118	P&O
472	HMS Abercrombie	Monitor	29 May 1915	6,180	Admiralty
473	HMS Havelock	Monitor	29 May 1915	6,180	Admiralty
474	Cancelled				
475	Cancelled				
476	HMS Raglan	Monitor	24 June 1915	6,180	Admiralty
477	HMS Prince Eugene	Monitor	2 September 1915	5,920	Admiralty
478	HMS Lord Clive	Monitor	10 July 1915	5,920	Admiralty
479	HMS General Craufurd	Monitor	26 August 1915	5,920	Admiralty
480	HMS Earl of Peterborough	Monitor	23 September 1915	5,920	Admiralty
481	HMS Sir Thomas Picton	Monitor	4 November 1915	5,920	Admiralty
482–484	HMS Glorious	Cruiser	31 December 1916	22,354	Admiralty

No.	Name	Type	Date Completed	Tonnage	Owner
485	HMS M29	Monitor	20 June 1915	360	Admiralty
486	HMS M30	Monitor	9 July 1915	360	Admiralty
487	HMS M31	Monitor	9 July 1915	360	Admiralty
488	HMS M32	Monitor	20 June 1915	360	Admiralty
489	HMS M33	Monitor	26 June 1915	360	Admiralty
490	HMS P24	Patrol boat	21 January 1916	616	Admiralty
491	HMS P25	Patrol boat	17 March 1916	616	Admiralty
492	HMS Erebus	Monitor	2 September 1916	8,022	Admiralty
493	HMS Terror	Monitor	6 August 1916	8,022	Admiralty
494	HMS Salmon	Destroyer	20 December 1916	1,121	Admiralty
495	HMS Sylph	Destroyer	10 February 1917	1,121	Admiralty
496	HMS Skilful	Destroyer	26 March 1917	1,121	Admiralty
497	HMS Springbok	Destroyer	30 April 1917	1,036	Admiralty
498	HMS Tenacious	Destroyer	11 August 1917	1,036	Admiralty
499	HMS Tetrarch	Destroyer	2 June 1917	1,036	Admiralty
500	HMS Vindictive	Seaplane carrier	19 October 1918	7,764	Admiralty
501	HMS P62	Patrol boat	31 August 1917	682	Admiralty
502	Glenogle	Cargo ship	19 August 1920	9,513	Glen Line
503	Glengarry	Cargo ship	23 February 1922	9,460	Glen Line
504	Glenapp	Cargo ship	14 December 1920	9,503	Glen Line
505	Glenbeg	Cargo ship	20 April 1922	9,464	Glen Line
506	Orova	Passenger ship	22 March 1923	12,257	PSNC
507	Asturias	Passenger ship	6 February 1926	22,048	Royal Mail
508	Lochkatrine	Passenger ship	18 January 1922	10,183	Royal Mail
509	Yorkshire	Passenger ship	2 September 1920	10,184	Bibby Steamship Co.
510	Coney	Coaster	27 April 1918	697	G. & J. Burns Ltd
511	Glenade	Cargo ship	16 July 1919	6,802	Glen Line
512	Glenariffe	Cargo ship	23 October 1919	6,795	Glen Line
513	Glentara	Cargo ship	13 April 1920	6,754	Glen Line
514	Glenluce	Cargo ship	14 January 1920	6,755	Glen Line
515	Dinteldyk	Cargo ship	10 February 1922	9,388	Holland-America Line
516	Lochgoil	Cargo ship	14 December 1922	9,462	Royal Mail
517	Lochmonar	Cargo ship	26 June 1924	9,463	Royal Mail
518	Cancelled				
519	Ekari	Cargo ship	13 April 1920	6,741	Elder Dempster
520	War Shamrock	A-type cargo ship	20 August 1917	5,174	Shipping Controller
521	War Clover	A Type	20 September 1917	5,174	Shipping Controller

No.	Name	Type	Date Completed	Tonnage	Owner
522	War Trefoil	A Type	16 October 1917	5,174	Shipping Controller
523	War Legate	AO Tanker	28 June 1918	5,188	Shipping Controller
524	War Envoy	AO Tanker	5 September 1918	5,197	Shipping Controller
525	War Hostage	AO Tanker	22 December 1917	5,181	Shipping Controller
526	War Expert	AO tanker	18 March 1918	5,198	Shipping Controller
527	War African	AO Tanker	15 May 1918	5,218	Shipping Controller
528	War Aryan	AO Tanker	7 November 1918	5,392	Shipping Controller
529	War Cowslip	A Type	13 December 1917	5,292	Shipping Controller
530	War Maple	AO Tanker	29 January 1920	5,281	Shipping Controller
531	War Viper	B-type cargo ship	14 March 1918	5,160	Shipping Controller
532	War Lemur	B Type	28 May 1918	5,185	Shipping Controller
533	War Cobra	B Type	20 December 1917	5,155	Shipping Controller
534	War Python	B Type	24 January 1918	5,155	Shipping Controller
535	War Bittern	B Type	11 April 1918	5,178	Shipping Controller
536	War Buckler	D-type cargo ship	30 May 1918	2,377	Shipping Controller
537	War Tabard	D Type	15 June 1918	2,357	Shipping Controller
538	War Snake	B Type	29 August 1918	5,222	Shipping Controller
539	War Poplar	B Type	25 November 1919	5,242	Shipping Controller
540	War Icarus	G-type cargo ship	31 October 1918	8,002	Shipping Controller
541	War Paris	G Type	17 April 1919	7,995	Shipping Controller
542	War Priam	G Type	13 March 1919	8,010	Shipping Controller
543	War Melody	N-type cargo ship	7 November 1918	6,533	Shipping Controller
544	War Music	N Type	5 December 1918	6,498	Shipping Controller
545	War Dream	N Type	9 January 1919	6,498	Shipping Controller
546	War Vision	N Type	8 May 1919	6,509	Shipping Controller

No.	Name	Type	Date Completed	Tonnage	Owner
547	War Triumph	A Type	7 October 1920	5,326	Shipping Controller
548	War Jasmine	A Type	31 December 1918	5,263	Shipping Controller
549	War Jonquil	A Type	9 September 1919	5,242	Shipping Controller
550	War Bamboo	A Type	19 November 1920	5,327	Shipping Controller
551	War Pampas	A Type	13 June 1919	5,256	Shipping Controller
552	HMS St Aubin	Tug	21 August 1918	468	Admiralty
553	HMS St Bees	Tug	24 October 1918	422	Admiralty
554	War Justice	N Type	27 May 1919	6,509	Shipping Controller
555	War Liberty	N Type	26 June 1919	6,529	Shipping Controller
556	New Georgia	N Type	14 August 1919	6,566	Elder Dempster
557	New Mexico	N Type	28 August 1919	6,566	Elder Dempster
558	New Toronto	N Type	9 October 1919	6,568	Elder Dempster
559	New Texas	N Type	18 September 1919	6,568	Elder Dempster
560	Bompata	B Type	16 January 1923	5,570	Elder Dempster
561	Boma	B Type	26 February 1920	5,407	Elder Dempster
562	Banda	Lighter	27 August 1926	70	Elder Dempster
563	HMS St Mellows	Tug	30 December 1918	421	Admiralty
564	HMS St Olaves	Tug	4 March 1919	468	Admiralty
565	War Riddle	N Type	4 March 1919	6,600	Atlantic Transport Co.
566	New Brooklyn	N Type	31 March 1920	6,573	Elder Dempster
567	New Columbia	N Type	30 June 1920	6,545	Atlantic Transport Co.
568	War Passion	N Type	23 March 1920	6,573	Elder Dempster
569	La Paz	Cargo ship	25 September 1920	5,327	PSNC
570	Biafra	B Type	19 June 1919	5,327	African Steamship Co.
571	Siris	B Type	25 September 1919	5,242	Royal Mail
572	Dundrum Castle	B Type	31 December 1919	5,242	Union Castle
573	Doric	Passenger ship	29 May 1923	16,484	OSNC
574	Philadelphian	N Type	19 February 1920	6,585	F. Leyland & Co.
575	Sophocles	Passenger ship	2 February 1922	12,361	George Thompson & Co.
576	Diogenes	Passenger ship	4 July 1922	12,341	George Thompson & Co.
577	New Brighton	N Type	31 January 1920	6,538	African Steamship Co.
578	Dorsetshire	Cargo ship	14 August 1920	7,445	Bibby Steamship Co.

No.	Name	Type	Date Completed	Tonnage	Owner
579	Somersetshire	Cargo ship	9 June 1921	7,456	Bibby Steamship Co.
580	Lobos	Cargo ship	14 October 1921	6,478	PSNC
581	Losada	Cargo ship	1 November 1921	6,520	PSNC
582	Ediba	Passenger ship	18 April 1923	6,919	African Steamship Co.
583	Baradine	Passenger ship	18 August 1921	13,143	P&O
584	Barrabool	Passenger ship	30 March 1922	13,143	P&O
585	Bendigo	Passenger ship	9 August 1922	13,039	P&O
586	Alcantara	Passenger ship	18 February 1927	22,181	Royal Mail
587	Mooltan	Passenger ship	22 September 1923	20,847	P&O
588	Maloja	Passenger ship	25 October 1923	20,837	P&O
589	Inverleith	Oil tanker	3 March 1921	6,957	British Mexican Petroleum Company (BMPC)
590	Inverurie	Oil tanker	23 November 1922	6,907	BMPC
591	Inveravon	Oil tanker	27 March 1923	6,906	BMPC
592	Somerset Coast	Coaster	25 March 1920	1,352	Coast Lines Ltd
593	Drechytk	Cargo ship	22 March 1923	9,324	Holland-America Line
594	Glenshiel	Cargo ship	22 May 1924	9,415	Glen Line
595	Carnarvon Castle	Passenger ship	26 June 1926	20,064	Union Castle
596	Calgary	Refrigerated cargo ship	3 February 1921	7,206	Elder Dempster
597	Cochrane	Refrigerated cargo ship	8 March 1923	7,203	Elder Dempster
598	Calumet	Refrigerated cargo ship	15 March 1923	7,268	Elder Dempster
599	Cariboo	Refrigerated cargo ship	16 August 1924	7,275	Elder Dempster
600	Lady Valentia	Coaster	16 November 1921	1,211	Coast Lines Ltd
601	Eastern Coast	Coaster	1 June 1922	1,223	Coast Lines Ltd
602	Redbreast	Coaster	11 February 1921	772	Coast Lines Ltd
603	Leighton	Cargo ship	13 October 1921	7,412	Lamport & Holt
604	Linnell	Cargo ship	27 December 1921	7,424	Lamport & Holt
605	Lassell	Cargo ship	22 June 1922	7,417	Lamport & Holt
606	Francunion	Oil barge	3 May 1921	737	British Union Oil Co.
607	Ayrshire Coast	Coaster	5 October 1922	773	Coast Lines Ltd
608	Adda	Passenger ship	14 November 1922	7,816	Elder Dempster
609	Invergarry	Oil tanker	17 April 1924	6,907	BMPC
610	Gujarat	Passenger ship	20 December 1923	4,184	Andrew Weir
611	Kathiawar	Passenger ship	15 February 1924	4,150	Andrew Weir

No.	Name	Type	Date Completed	Tonnage	Owner
612	Statendam	Passenger ship	13 April 1923	28,130	Holland-America Line
613	Minnewaska	Passenger ship	25 August 1923	21,716	Atlantic Transport Co.
614	Minnetonka	Passenger ship	24 April 1924	21,998	Atlantic Transport Co.
615	Oakton	Cargo ship	31 May 1923	1,727	Matthews Steamship Co.
616	Accra	Passenger ship	17 August 1926	9,337	Elder Dempster
617	Britmex No. 2	Oil barge	16 June 1920	474	Andrew Weir
618	Britmex No. 3	Oil barge	17 June 1920	474	Andrew Weir
619	Btitmex No. 4	Oil barge	4 June 1920	474	Andrew Weir
620	Britmex No. 5	Oil barge	1 July 1920	475	Andrew Weir
621	Britmex No. 6	Oil barge	28 May 1920	475	Andrew Weir
622	Britmex No. 7	Oil barge	3 June 1920	475	Andrew Weir
623	Britmex No. 8	Oil barge	8 June 1920	475	Andrew Weir
624	Inveritchen	Oil tanker	1 October 1920	708	BMPC
625	Inverampton	Oil tanker	1 November 1920	708	BMPC
626	Gorilla	Coaster	7 February 1922	772	Coast Lines Ltd
627	Dorelian	Cargo ship	15 May 1923	6,300	F. Leyland & Co.
628	Cancelled				
629	Cancelled				
630	Araby	Cargo ship	16 March 1923	4,936	David MacIver & Co.
631	Cedarton	Cargo ship	5 April 1924	899	Matthews Steamship Co.
632	Laguna	Cargo ship	3 July 1923	6,469	PSNC
633	Tonbridge	Ferry	21 July 1924	682	Southern Railway Co.
634	Minster	Ferry	18 August 1924	682	Southern Railway Co.
635	Ulster Monarch	Ferry	10 June 1929	3,851	Belfast Steamship Co.
636	Elmsworth	Cargo ship	13 November 1924	4,963	R.S. Dalglish Ltd
637	Oakworth	Cargo ship	12 February 1925	4,963	R.S. Dalglish Ltd
638	Ferry No. 6	Ferry	7 November 1922	16	Clyde Navigation Co.
639	Ferry No. 7	Ferry	7 November 1922	16	Clyde Navigation Co.
640	Inverglass	Oil tanker	25 November 1924	6,901	BMPC
641	Invergoil	Oil tanker	9 November 1922	6,966	BMPC
642	Luxmi	Passenger ship	25 March 1924	4,184	Andrew Weir
643	Inverbank	Cargo ship	29 May 1924	5,149	Andrew Weir
644	Invergordon	Oil tanker	5 April 1923	6,921	BMPC

No.	Name	Type	Date Completed	Tonnage	Owner
645	Unnamed	Floating dock	12 April 1923	589	Harland and Wolff
646	Grantleyhall	Cargo ship	16 August 1927	4,761	West Hartlepool Steamship Co.
647	Birchton	Cargo ship	12 April 1924	1,732	Matthews Steamship Co.
648	Cable Enterprise	Cable layer	20 May 1924	943	Western Telegraph Co.
649	Volendam	Passenger ship	12 October 1922	15,440	Holland-America Line
650	Veendam	Passenger ship	29 March 1923	15,450	Holland-America Line
651	Britmex No. 1	Oil barge	26 November 1920	472	BMPC
652	Britmex No. 9	Oil barge	23 December 1920	471	BMPC
653	Britmex No. 10	Oil barge	7 March 1921	475	BMPC
654	Britmex No. 11	Oil barge	8 March 1921	475	BMPC
655	Glenbank	Cargo ship	27 June 1924	5,150	Andrew Weir
656	Birchbank	Cargo ship	4 September 1924	5,150	Andrew Weir
657	Lurcher	Coaster	11 November 1922	774	Coast Lines Ltd
658	Asuka Maru	Cargo ship	12 November 1924	7,488	Nippon Yusen Kaisha Line
659	Razmak	Passenger ship	26 February 1925	10,602	P&O
660	Rawalpindi	Passenger ship	3 September 1925	16,618	P&O
661	Pajputana	Passenger ship	30 December 1925	16,585	P&O
662	Cedarbank	Cargo ship	16 October 1924	5,151	Andrew Weir
663	Comliebank	Cargo ship	6 December 1924	5,149	Andrew Weir
664	Clydebank	Cargo ship	2 January 1925	5,156	Andrew Weir
665–674	Unnamed	Barges	August/September 1923	50	Elder Dempster
675	Thistleros	Cargo ship	19 March 1925	4,615	Allan Black & Co.
676	Alynbank	Cargo ship	26 March 1925	5,151	Andrew Weir
677	Elmbank	Cargo ship	23 April 1925	5,155	Andrew Weir
678	Forrestbank	Cargo ship	11 June 1925	5,155	Andrew Weir
679	Nairnbank	Cargo ship	7 July 1925	5,156	Andrew Weir
680	Weirbank	Cargo ship	9 September 1925	5,150	Andrew Weir
681	Larchbank	Cargo ship	1 October 1925	5,150	Andrew Weir
682	Levernbank	Cargo ship	23 November 1925	5,150	Andrew Weir
683	Myrtlebank	Cargo ship	29 December 1925	5,150	Andrew Weir
684	Olivebank	Cargo ship	9 February 1926	5,154	Andrew Weir
685	Oakbank	Cargo ship	11 March 1926	5,154	Andrew Weir
686	Speybank	Cargo ship	20 April 1926	5,155	Andrew Weir
687	Springbank	Cargo ship	26 may 1926	5,155	Andrew Weir
688	Procris	Cargo ship	27 November 1924	1,320	J. & P. Hutchinson Ltd

No.	Name	Type	Date Completed	Tonnage	Owner
689	Fendris	Cargo ship	5 February 1925	1,320	J. & P. Hutchinson Ltd
690	Paupan Chief	Cargo ship	24 September 1924	255	Steamship Trading Co.
691	King James	Cargo ship	28 November 1925	5,065	King Line
692	King Malcolm	Cargo ship	29 December 1925	5,064	King Line
693	Temuco	Tender	22 September 1925	125	P&O
695	Apapa	Passenger ship	28 January 1927	9,350	Elder Dempster
696	Ulster Queen	Ferry	11 February 1930	3,756	Belfast Steamship Co.
697	Ulster Prince	Ferry	3 March 1930	3,756	Belfast Steamship Co.
698	Redline No. 1	Oil tanker	5 November 1924	272	BMPC
699	Inverlago	Oil tanker	24 March 1925	2,372	Lago Shipping Co.
700	Inverossa	Oil tanker	24 April 1925	2,372	Lago Shipping Co.
701	Invercaibo	Oil tanker	9 June 1925	2,372	Lago Shipping Co.
702	Inverruba	Oil tanker	30 June 1925	2,372	Lago Shipping Co.
703	Waterman	Water barge	21 January 1925	260	Andrew Weir
704	Madrid	Cargo ship	30 December 1925	1,453	Argentine Navigation Co.
705	Roma	Cargo ship	24 February 1926	1,455	Argentine Navigation Co.
706	Hythe	Ferry	5 June 1925	685	Southern Railway Co.
707	Whitstable	Ferry	17 August 1925	685	Southern Railway Co.
708	Inverpool	Oil tanker	20 May 1925	680	BMPC
709	Marthara	Cargo ship	16 January 1926	4,999	MacLay & MacIntyre Ltd
710–715	Unnamed	Barge	March/April 1926	150	Andrew Weir
716	Gascony	Cargo ship	25 November 1925	4,716	David MacIver & Co.
717–718	Unnamed	Barges	17 March 1925	80	Andrew Weir
719	Hazelmere	Ferry	6 July 1925	756	Southern Railway Co.
720	Fratton	Ferry	28 September 1925	757	Southern Railway Co.
721	Colonial	Cargo ship	19 February 1926	5,108	T. & J. Harrison
722	Director	Cargo ship	8 March 1926	5,107	T. & J. Harrison
723–724	Unnamed	Lighters	28 September 1925	48	Elder Dempster

No.	Name	Type	Date Completed	Tonnage	Owner
725	Dolores de Urquiza	Train ferry	2 October 1926	2,217	Entre Rios Railway Co.
726–727	Unnamed	Barges	29 October 1926	75	Andrew Weir
728	Koolinda	Cargo ship	23 December 1926	4,372	Western Australian Government
729	Maidstone	Ferry	30 April 1926	688	Southern Railway Co.
730	Ringwood	Ferry	14 June 1926	755	Southern Railway Co.
731	London Mammoth	Crane pontoon	16 July 1927	1,580	Port of London Authority
732	Begonia	Oil barge	26 April 1926	814	Argentine Navigation Co.
733	Boltonia	Oil barge	28 April 1926	814	Argentine Navigation Co.
734	George Livesey	Tug	12 May 1928	107	Southern Gas Company
735	Dunkwa	Cargo ship	24 August 1927	3,789	Elder Dempster
736	Dixcove	Cargo ship	21 October 1927	3,787	Elder Dempster
737	Daru	Cargo ship	20 December 1927	3,838	Elder Dempster
738	Dagomba	Cargo ship	15 March 1928	3,845	Elder Dempster
739	San Nicolas	Oil tanker	20 May 1926	2,391	Lago Shipping Co.
740	Papudo	Tug	2 June 1926	47	PSNC
741	Palacio	Cargo ship	19 October 1927	1,346	MacAndrews & Co.
742	Pelayo	Cargo ship	1 December 1927	1,346	MacAndrews & Co.
743	Pacheco	Cargo ship	22 December 1927	1,346	MacAndrews & Co.
744	Pinto	Cargo ship	2 February 1928	1,346	MacAndrews & Co.
745	Ponzano	Cargo ship	28 February 1928	1,346	MacAndrews & Co.
746	Ambrosio	Oil tanker	7 July 1926	2,391	Lago Shipping Co.
747	Petronella	Oil tanker	11 October 1927	2,770	Nederland Stoomboot Co.
748	Paula	Oil tanker	22 November 1927	2,770	Nederland Stoomboot Co.
749	Agatha	Oil tanker	8 September 1927	2,770	Nederland Stoomboot Co.
750	Paua	Oil Tanker	9 June 1927	2,770	Nederland Stoomboot Co.
751	Highland Monarch	Passenger ship	2 October 1928	14,137	H. & W. Nelson Ltd

No.	Name	Type	Date Completed	Tonnage	Owner
752	Sin Kheng Seng	Coaster	2 April 1927	200	McKie & Baxter Ltd
753	Unnamed	Floating dock	2 December 1926	260	Entre Rios Railway Co.
754	La Falaise	Yacht	13 July 1927	119	Mr James Allen
755	Unnamed	Dock gate	12 February 1927	83	Montevideo Drydock Co.
756	Minmi	Coaster	30 June 1927	1,455	J. & A. Brown Ltd
757	King Edgar	Cargo ship	30 November 1927	4,536	King Line
758	King Edwin	Cargo ship	20 December 1927	4,536	King Line
759	King Egbert	Cargo ship	17 January 1928	4,536	King Line
760	King John	Cargo ship	16 February 1928	5,228	King Line
761	King Lud	Cargo ship	15 March 1928	5,228	King Line
762	King Neptune	Cargo ship	17 April 1928	5,224	King Line
763	King Arthur	Cargo ship	17 May 1928	5,224	King Line
764	King Stephen	Cargo ship	14 June 1928	5,274	King Line
765	King William	Cargo ship	19 May 1928	5,273	King Line
766–779	Unnamed	Barges	29 December 1926	80	Andrew Weir
780	Encina	Lighter	9 May 1927	165	Argentine Navigation Co.
781	Enea	Lighter	24 May 1927	165	Argentine Navigation Co.
782	Erata	Lighter	5 July 1927	165	Argentine Navigation Co.
783	Erica	Lighter	5 July 1927	165	Argentine Navigation Co.
784–785	Unnamed	Barges	21 April 1927	80	Andrew Weir
786	Portwey	Tug	28 April 1928	94	Portland & Weymouth Coaling Company
787	Eddystone	Coaster	15 September 1927	1,550	Clyde Shipping Co.
788–790	Unnamed	Barges	20 June 1927	56	Elder Dempster
791	Uganda	Cargo ship	4 November 1927	4,966	MacLay & MacIntyre Ltd
792	Lagunilla	Oil tanker	16 June 1927	2,402	Lago Shipping Co.
793	Icotea	Oil tanker	17 June 1927	2,402	Lago Shipping Co.
794	La Salina	Oil tanker	28 June 1927	2,402	Lago Shipping Co.
795	San Carlos	Oil tanker	29 July 1927	2,395	Lago Shipping Co.

No.	Name	Type	Date Completed	Tonnage	Owner
796	Lahji	Tug	16 October 1927	283	P&O
797	Nimoda	Cargo ship	19 January 1928	4,736	Hain Steamship Co.
798	Berta	Oil tanker	14 July 1927	2,611	Anglo Saxon Petroleum Co.
799	Brigida	Oil tanker	30 August 1927	2,609	Anglo Saxon Petroleum Co.
800	Kheti	Cargo ship	25 October 1927	2,650	James Moss Ltd
801	Saugor	Cargo ship	29 March 1928	6,303	James Nourse Ltd
802	Cabo Espichel	Tug	28 March 1928	304	McKie & Baxter Ltd
803	Cabo Raso	Tug	2 August 1928	230	McKie & Baxter Ltd
804	Cabo Sardao	Tug	17 August 1928	230	McKie & Baxter Ltd
805	Iguazu	Passenger ship	26 November 1927	523	Argentine Navigation Co.
806	Highland Chieftain	Passenger ship	26 January 1929	14,130	H. & W. Nelson Ltd
807	Britannic	Passenger ship	21 June 1930	26,934	OSNC
808	Clydefield	Oil tanker	12 July 1928	6,758	Hunting & Sons
809	Oranjestad	Oil tanker	23 September 1927	2,396	Andrew Weir
810	Sabaneta	Oil tanker	30 September 1927	2,396	Andrew Weir
811	Zahra	Oil tanker	22 November 1927	821	Vacuum Oil Company
812	Highland Brigade	Passenger ship	27 April 1929	14,131	H. & W. Nelson Ltd
813	Highland Hope	Passenger ship	26 January 1930	14,129	H. & W. Nelson Ltd
814	Highland Princess	Passenger ship	25 February 1930	14,128	H. & W. Nelson Ltd
815	Delfina Mitre	Train ferry	29 May 1928	2,235	Entre Rios railway Co.
816	Dafila	Cargo ship	10 January 1928	1,940	British & Continental Steamship Co.
817	Nyanza	Cargo ship	4 July 1928	4,974	MacLay & MacIntyre Ltd
818	Deal	Ferry	20 March 1928	688	Southern Railway Co.
819–822	Unnamed	Tugs	6 October 1927	29	Lago Shipping Co.
823	Unnamed	Oil barge	1 November 1927	110	Burmah Oil Company
824	Brittany	Cargo ship	30 June 1928	4,772	David MacIver & Co.
825	Winchester Castle	Passenger ship	11 October 1930	20,108	Union Castle

No.	Name	Type	Date Completed	Tonnage	Owner
826	Designer	Cargo ship	7 September 1928	5,945	T. & J. Harrison Ltd
827	Sefwi	Barge	29 November 1927	57	Elder Dempster
828	Wala	Barge	29 November 1927	57	Elder Dempster
829	Cuidad de Salto	Passenger ship	21 September 1928	1,952	Argentine Navigation Co.
830	Behar	Cargo ship	7 November 1928	6,100	Hain Steamship Co.
831	Kerma	Cargo ship	20 September 1928	4,333	Strick Line
832	Punta Benitez	Oil tanker	16 March 1928	2,394	Lago Shipping Co.
833	Tia Juana	Oil tanker	4 April 1928	2,395	Lago Shipping Co.
834	Hooberg	Oil tanker	25 April 1928	2,395	Lago Shipping Co.
835	Punta Gorda	Oil tanker	18 May 1928	2,395	Lago Shipping Co.
836	Yamanota	Oil tanker	13 June 1928	2,395	Lago Shipping Co.
837	Celtic Monarch	Cargo ship	7 January 1929	5,822	Raeburn & Verel Ltd
838	Centura	Lighter	12 July 1928	788	Argentine Navigation Co.
839	Unnamed	Barge	19 September 1928	110	Burmah Oil Company
840	Warwick Castle	Passenger ship	16 January 1931	20,444	Union Castle
841	Llangibby Castle	Passenger ship	21 November 1929	11,951	Union Castle
842	Bhutan	Cargo ship	13 March 1929	6,104	Hain Steamship Co.
843	Westrailia	Refrigerated cargo ship	15 August 1929	8,107	Huddart Parker
844	Cancelled				
845	Cardiff	Cargo ship	7 March 1929	1,483	Argentine Navigation Co.
846	Glasgow	Cargo ship	24 April 1929	1,483	Argentine Navigation Co.
847	Ciudad de Ascuncion	Cargo ship	17 March 1930	2,851	Argentine Navigation Co.
848	Ciudad de Corrientes	Cargo ship	14 October 1930	2,854	Argentine Navigation Co.
849	Wanganella	Passenger ship	29 November 1932	9,576	Huddart Parker
850	Idomo	Lighter	10 January 1929	55	Elder Dempster
851	Dunbar Castle	Passenger ship	20 May 1930	10,002	Union Castle
852	Reina del Pacifico	Passenger ship	24 March 1931	17,707	PSNC
853	David Livingstone	Cargo ship	20 March 1930	4,022	British & African Steamship Co.
854	Mary Slessor	Cargo ship	23 April 1930	4,016	British & African Steamship Co.

No.	Name	Type	Date Completed	Tonnage	Owner
855	William Wilberforce	Cargo ship	10 May 1930	4,013	British & African Steamship Co.
856	Baron Vernon	Cargo ship	28 June 1929	3,642	H. Hogarth & Sons
857	Baron Ramsey	Cargo ship	12 July 1929	3,650	H. Hogarth & Sons
858	Kaufra	Cargo ship	19 November 1929	2,608	James Moss & Co.
859	Irwin	Ferry	2 September 1929	970	South India Railways
860	Goschen	Ferry	20 September 1929	970	South India Railways
861	Tamare	Oil tanker	7 May 1929	3,046	Lago Shipping Co.
862	Tasajeras	Oil tanker	20 May 1929	3,046	Lago Shipping Co.
863	Surinam	Oil tanker	29 May 1929	3,046	Lago Shipping Co.
864	Kavak	Cargo ship	19 September 1929	2,734	Moss Steamship Co.
865	Kana	Cargo ship	1 November 1929	2,734	Moss Steamship Co.
866	Carmen Avellaneda	Train ferry	13 December 1929	2,234	Entre Rios Railways Co.
867	Edward Blyden	Cargo ship	29 May 1930	4,022	British & African Steamship Co.
868	Alfred Jones	Cargo ship	20 August 1930	4,022	British & African Steamship Co.
869	Macgregor Laird	Cargo ship	3 July 1930	4,022	British & African Steamship Co.
870	Innisfallen	Ferry	14 June 1930	3,019	City of Cork Steam Packet Co.
871	Ardanbhan	Cargo ship	7 November 1929	777	Clarke & Service Ltd
872	Loch Ness	Ferry	9 July 1929	1,200	David MacBrayne & Co.
873	Ambers	Cargo ship	25 March 1930	1,497	Argentine Navigation Co.
874	Barcelona	Cargo ship	16 April 1930	1,497	Argentine Navigation Co.
875	Genova	Cargo ship	27 May 1930	1,497	Argentine Navigation Co.
876	Hamburgo	Cargo ship	17 September 1930	1,497	Argentine Navigation Co.
877	Guayra	Ferry	14 November 1930	1,850	Argentine Navigation Co.
878	Foylebank	Cargo ship	10 November 1930	5,582	Andrew Weir
879	Laganbank	Cargo ship	11 December 1930	5,582	Andrew Weir
880	Dorothy Rose	Cargo ship	21 November 1930	1,600	Richard Hughes & Co.

No.	Name	Type	Date Completed	Tonnage	Owner
881	Dudley Rose	Cargo ship	23 December 1930	1,600	Richard Hughes & Co.
882	Silvercypress	Cargo ship	18 June 1930	6,770	Silver Line Ltd
883	Silverwalnut	Cargo ship	23 July 1930	6,770	Silver Line Ltd
884	Silverteak	Cargo ship	2 September 1930	6,770	Silver Line Ltd
885	Silversandal	Cargo ship	19 September 1930	6,770	Silver Line Ltd
886	Baron Napier	Cargo ship	21 March 1930	3,659	H. Hogarth & Sons
887	Baron Erskine	Cargo ship	17 April 1930	3,659	H. Hogarth & Sons
888	San Antonio	Cargo ship	24 September 1930	5,986	Compagnie General Transatlantique
889	San Diego	Cargo ship	11 November 1930	5,986	Compagnie General Transatlantique
890	San Francisco	Cargo ship	10 December 1930	5,984	Compagnie General Transatlantique
891	San Jose	Cargo ship	23 January 1931	5,982	Compagnie General Transatlantique
892	San Mateo	Cargo ship	6 March 1931	5,935	Compagnie General Transatlantique
893	San Pedro	Cargo ship	17 April 1931	5,935	Compagnie General Transatlantique
894	Ciudad de Concepcion	Ferry	25 January 1930	897	Argentine Navigation Co.
895	Unnamed	Lighter	25 March 1930	900	Argentine Navigation Co.
896	Georgic	Passenger ship	10 June 1932	27,267	OSNC
897	Ganges	Cargo ship	29 October 1930	6,253	James Nourse Ltd
898	Somali	Cargo ship	18 December 1930	6,809	Hain Shipping Co.
899	Ebano	Asphalt carrier	30 October 1930	2,697	Ebano Oil Co.
900	Prestatyn Rose	Cargo ship	20 May 1930	1,151	Richard Hughes & Co.
901	Anglesea Rose	Cargo ship	7 June 1930	1,151	Richard Hughes & Co.
902	Medoc	Cargo ship	26 June 1930	1,166	Worms & Co.
903	Pomerol	Cargo ship	8 July 1930	1,167	Worms & Co.
904	Chateau Larose	Cargo ship	23 August 1930	2,047	Worms & Co.
905	Chateau Pavie	Cargo ship	11 September 1930	2,047	Worms & Co.
906	Maurice Rose	Cargo ship	24 October 1930	1,600	Richard Hughes & Co.
907	Dennis Rose	Cargo ship	7 November 1930	1,600	Richard Hughes & Co.

No.	Name	Type	Date Completed	Tonnage	Owner
908	Cliona	Oil tanker	14 October 1931	8,375	Anglo Saxon Petroleum Co.
909	Conch	Oil tanker	22 December 1931	8,376	Anglo Saxon Petroleum Co.
910	Rockabill	Coaster	29 January 1931	1,392	Clyde Shipping Co.
911	Triona	Cargo ship	21 March 1931	4,413	British Phosphate Carriers
912	Aurocarrier	Ferry	26 March 1931	822	Southern Railways
913	Ogeni	Paddle steamer	17 April 1931	47	Elder Dempster
914	East Goodwin	Lightship	13 April 1932	260	Trinity House
915	Maracay	Oil tanker	16 June 1931	3,795	Lago Shipping Co.
916	Highland Patriot	Passenger ship	15 May 1932	14,156	Nelson Steamship Co.
917	Unnamed	Crane pontoon	20 August 1932	608	Cowan & Sheldon Ltd
918	Royal Iris II	Ferry	12 May 1932	607	Wallasey Corporation
919	Baron Ardrossan	Cargo ship	4 June 1932	3,896	H. Hogarth & Sons
920	Duchess of Hamilton	Clyde steamer	24 June 1932	795	Caledonian Steam Packet Co.
921	North Carr	Lightship	27 February 1933	268	Trinity House
922	Waiwera	Refrigerated cargo ship	29 August 1934	10,781	Shaw Savill
923	Waipawa	Refrigerated cargo ship	19 October 1934	10,784	Shaw Savill
924	Wairangi	Refrigerated cargo ship	26 January 1935	10,779	Shaw Savill
925	Bhadravati	Ferry	10 September 1932	1,306	Bombay Steam Navigation Co.
926	Chandravati	Ferry	31 August 1933	557	Bombay Steam Navigation Co.
927	Baron Dunmore	Cargo ship	22 September 1933	3,938	H. Hogarth & Sons
928	Baron Elgin	Cargo ship	4 October 1933	3,942	H. Hogarth & Sons
929	Prabhavati	Ferry	28 September 1933	556	Bombay Steam Navigation Co.
930	Idalia	Yacht	2 July 1934	147	Alan F. Craig
931	Loch Lomond	Cargo ship	21 September 1934	5,452	MacLay & MacIntyre Ltd
932	Anadara	Oil tanker	28 February 1935	8,008	Anglo Saxon Petroleum Co.
933	Imperial Star	Refrigerated cargo ship	29 December 1934	10,733	Blue Star Line
934	New Zealand Star	Refrigerated cargo ship	1 March 1935	10,740	Blue Star Line

No.	Name	Type	Date Completed	Tonnage	Owner
935	Sir Hastings Anderson	Target towing vessel	12 September 1934	228	Admiralty
936	John Dock	Tug	9 October 1934	551	South African Railways
937	W.H. Fuller	Tug	9 November 1934	552	South African Railways
938	San Arcadio	Oil tanker	17 April 1935	7,419	Eagle Oil Co.
939	Australia Star	Refrigerated cargo ship	17 April 1935	11,122	Blue Star Line
940	HMS Penelope	Cruiser	15 November 1936	5,050	Admiralty
941	Sterling Castle	Passenger ship	29 January 1936	25,594	Union Castle
942	Athlone Castle	Passenger ship	13 May 1936	25,567	Union Castle
943	Roslin Castle	Refrigerated cargo ship	4 May 1935	7,016	Union Castle
944	Rothesay Castle	Refrigerated cargo ship	11 May 1935	7,016	Union Castle
945	Henzada	Cargo ship	22 November 1934	4,161	P. Henderson & Co.
946	Martaban	Cargo ship	26 December 1934	4,161	P. Henderson & Co.
947	Baron Renfrew	Cargo ship	3 March 1935	3,635	H. Hogarth & Sons
948	Baron Cawdor	Cargo ship	16 January 1935	3,638	H. Hogarth & Sons
949	Flying Falcon	Tug	15 September 1934	283	Clyde Shipping Co.
950	Saganaga	Cargo ship	15 April 1935	5,454	Christian Salvasen & Co.
951	Duke of York	Ferry	4 June 1936	3,759	LMS Railways
952	Mpasa	Coaster	1 February 1935	270	Nyasaland Railways
953	Inventor	Cargo ship	11 September 1935	6,210	T. & J. Harrison
954	Calabar	Passenger ship	19 March 1935	1,932	Elder Dempster
955	Kanimbala	Passenger ship	26 April 1935	10,984	McIlwrath & McEachern Ltd
956	Talisman	Ferry	12 June 1935	544	London & North Eastern Railway
957	Empire Star	Refrigerated cargo ship	20 December 1935	11,093	Blue Star Line
958	Sydney Star	Refrigerated cargo ship	19 March 1936	11,095	Blue Star Line
959	Dunnottar Castle	Passenger ship	27 June 1936	15,007	Union Castle
960	Dunvegan Castle	Passenger ship	27 August 1936	15,007	Union Castle
961	Standella	Oil tanker	16 April 1936	6,197	Anglo Saxon Petroleum Co.
962	Simnia	Oil tanker	14 May 1936	6,197	Anglo Saxon Petroleum Co.
963	Royal Ulsterman	Ferry	13 June 1936	3,290	Burns & Laird Line

No.	Name	Type	Date Completed	Tonnage	Owner
964	Royal Scotsman	Ferry	29 May 1936	3,290	Burns & Laird Line
965	Sonavati	Ferry	21 February 1936	1,663	Bombay Steam Navigation Co.
966	Eros	Fruit carrier	8 April 1936	5,888	Erin Steamship Co.
967	Duchess of Abercorn	Ferry	17 March 1936	308	Belfast Harbour Commissioners
968	British Power	Oil tanker	16 December 1936	8,334	British Tanker Company
969	British Destiny	Oil tanker	21 January 1937	8,334	British Tanker Company
970	Adelong	Cargo ship	18 July 1936	3,576	Huddart Parker
971	Boardale	Oil tanker	7 June 1937	8,334	British Tanker Company
972	British Integrity	Oil tanker	8 September 1937	8,334	British Tanker Company
973	Broomdale	Oil tanker	3 November 1927	8,334	British Tanker Company
974	British Security	Oil tanker	29 December 1937	8,334	British Tanker Company
975	Charles McIver	Trawler	17 July 1936	500	Lancashire Sea Fisheries Ltd
976	Lairdswood	Livestock carrier	15 August 1936	789	Burns & Laird Line
977	Lairdscrest	Livestock carrier	26 August 1936	789	Burns & Laird Line
978	Lairdsbank	Livestock carrier	24 September 1936	789	Burns & Laird Line
979	Cameo	Coaster	3 February 1937	946	William Robertson Ltd
980	Delius	Cargo ship	6 July 1937	6,065	Lamport & Holt
981	Sitala	Oil tanker	10 March 1937	6,218	Anglo Saxon Petroleum Co.
982	Salacia	Cargo ship	17 August 1937	5,495	Donaldson Lin Ltd
983	Walmer Castle	Cargo ship	30 November 1936	905	Union Castle
984	Ernebank	Cargo ship	18 February 1937	5,388	Andrew Weir
985	Dipavati	Ferry	17 September 1936	840	Bombay Steam Navigation Co.
986	Capetown Castle	Passenger ship	31 March 1938	27,002	Union Castle
987	Durban Castle	Passenger ship	15 December 1938	17,388	Union Castle
988	Crossgar	Collier	28 November 1936	661	John Kelly Ltd
989	Leonora	Tug	15 July 1936	86	McKie & Baxter Ltd
990	Comara	Coaster	7 April 1937	751	North Coast Steam Navigation Company
991	May	Lightship tender	30 March 1937	491	Commissioners of Irish Lights
992	Rochester Castle	Refrigerated cargo ship	29 April 1937	7,795	Union Castle

No.	Name	Type	Date Completed	Tonnage	Owner
993	Roxburgh Castle	Refrigerated cargo ship	26 June 1937	7,800	Union Castle
994	Torr Head	Cargo ship	10 April 1937	5,021	Ulster Steamship Co.
995	Leinster	Ferry	2 November 1937	4,302	British & Irish Steam Packet Co.
996	Munster	Ferry	22 February 1938	4,302	British & Irish Steam Packet Co.
997	Lady Sylvia	Ferry	8 May 1937	199	Union Steamship Co.
998	Donaghadee	Collier	9 September 1937	662	John Kelly Ltd
999	Loch Avon	Cargo ship	29 July 1938	9,204	Royal Mail
1000	HMS Belfast	Cruiser	3 August 1939	10,173	Admiralty
1001	Delane	Cargo ship	17 January 1938	6,054	Lamport & Holt
1002	Devis	Cargo ship	14 February 1938	6,054	Lamport & Holt
1003	Koolama	Cargo ship	2 April 1938	4,026	Western Australian Government
1004	Waimarama	Cargo ship	6 October 1938	11,091	Shaw Savill
1005	Andes	Passenger ship	24 September 1939	25,668	Royal Mail
1006	Pretoria Castle	Passenger ship	18 April 1939	17,382	Union Castle
1007	HMS Formidable	Aircraft carrier	24 November 1940	28,094	Admiralty
1008	Donax	Oil tanker	28 April 1938	8,036	Anglo Saxon Petroleum Co.
1009	Dromus	Oil tanker	14 September 1938	8,036	Anglo Saxon Petroleum Co.
1010	British Fidelity	Oil tanker	26 October 1938	8,465	British Tanker Co.
1011	British Trust	Oil tanker	19 January 1938	8,465	British Tanker Co.
1012	Richmond Castle	Refrigerated cargo ship	11 February 1939	7,798	Union Castle
1013	Rowallan Castle	Refrigerated cargo ship	11 March 1939	7,798	Union Castle
1014	Cairndale	Oil tanker	26 January 1939	8,129	Admiralty
1015	San Emiliano	Oil tanker	5 April 1939	8,071	Eagle Oil Company
1016	Wellington Star	Refrigerated cargo ship	24 August 1939	12,382	Blue Star Line
1017	Auckland Star	Refrigerated cargo ship	4 November 1939	12,382	Blue Star Line
1018	Bangalow	Coaster	15 March 1939	632	North Coast Navigation Co.
1019	Waiotira	Passenger ship	24 November 1939	11,102	Shaw Savill
1020	Theodor Woker	Tug	23 May 1939	620	Government of South Africa
1021	Watermayer	Tug	1 November 1939	620	Government of South Africa

No.	Name	Type	Date Completed	Tonnage	Owner
1022	Degei	Ferry	18 April 1939	205	Government of Fiji
1023	HMS Adamant	Submarine depot ship	28 February 1942	12,500	Admiralty
1024	Lincoln Castle	Paddle steamer	4 July 1941	598	London & North Eastern Railway
1025	Pardo	Refrigerated cargo ship	15 August 1940	5,400	Royal Mail
1026	Potaro	Refrigerated cargo ship	19 November 1940	5,409	Royal Mail
1027	Pampas	Refrigerated cargo ship	23 January 1941	5,419	Royal Mail
1028	Palma	Refrigerated cargo ship	2 April 1941	5,419	Royal Mail
1029	Debrett	Cargo ship	23 May 1940	8,104	Lamport & Holt
1030	Defoe	Cargo ship	30 August 1940	6,245	Lamport & Holt
1031	HMS Unicorn	Aircraft maintenance carrier	12 March 1943	14,750	Admiralty
1032	Lavington Court	Cargo ship	26 June 1940	5,372	Court Line Ltd
1033	Novelist	Cargo ship	8 August 1940	6,133	T. & J. Harrison
1034	Araybank	Cargo ship	24 October 1940	7,258	Andrew Weir
1035	Shirrabank	Cargo ship	5 December 1940	7,274	Andrew Weir
1036	Fanad Head	Cargo ship	19 December 1940	5,038	Ulster Steamship Co.
1037	HMS Elm	Tree-class trawler	9 March 1940	530	Admiralty
1038	HMS Fir	Tree-class trawler	30 April 1940	530	Admiralty
1039	HMS Bangor	Bangor-class minesweeper	4 November 1940	656	Admiralty
1040	HMS Blackpool	Bangor-class minesweeper	7 February 1941	656	Admiralty
1041	HMS Coreopsis	Flower-class corvette	17 August 1940	925	Admiralty
1042	HMS Crocus	Flower-class corvette	26 June 1940	925	Admiralty
1043	Vipya	Ferry	23 October 1942	270	Nyasaland Railway Co.
1044	HMS Dingledale	Oil tanker	10 September 1941	8,145	Admiralty
1045	Empire Gem	Oil tanker	24 October 1941	8,139	Admiralty
1046	HMS Black Ranger	Oil tanker	27 January 1941	3,417	Admiralty
1047	HMS Blue Ranger	Oil tanker	6 June 1941	3,417	Admiralty
1048	HMS Brown Ranger	Oil tanker	11 April 1941	3,417	Admiralty
1049	HMS Black Prince	Cruiser	20 November 1943	5,950	Admiralty
1050	Empire Hope	Refrigerated cargo ship	22 October 1941	12,688	Ministry of Supply

No.	Name	Type	Date Completed	Tonnage	Owner
1051	Empire Grace	Refrigerated cargo ship	1 April 1942	13,487	Ministry of Supply
1052	Derwentdale	Landing ship	30 August 1941	8,389	Admiralty
1053	Empire Diamond	Oil tanker	12 November 1941	8,236	Ministry of Supply
1054	HMS Rumba	Dance-class trawler	12 November 1940	530	Admiralty
1055	HMS Sarabande	Dance-class trawler	2 January 1941	530	Admiralty
1056	HMS Spirea	Flower-class corvette	27 February 1941	724	Admiralty
1057	HMS Starwort	Flower-class corvette	26 May 1941	724	Admiralty
1058	HMS Arabis	Flower-class corvette	5 April 1940	724	Admiralty
1059	HMS Periwinkle	Flower-class corvette	8 April 1940	724	Admiralty
1060	HMS Clarkia	Flower-class corvette	22 April 1940	724	Admiralty
1061	HMS Calendula	Flower-class corvette	6 May 1940	724	Admiralty
1062	HMS Hibiscus	Flower-class corvette	21 May 1940	724	Admiralty
1063	HMS Heartsease	Flower-class corvette	4 June 1940	724	Admiralty
1064	HMS Camellia	Flower-class corvette	18 June 1940	724	Admiralty
1065	HMS Mallow	Flower-class corvette	2 July 1940	722	Admiralty
1066	HMS Peony	Flower-class corvette	2 August 1940	722	Admiralty
1067	HMS Erica	Flower-class corvette	9 August 1940	722	Admiralty
1068	HMS Gloxinia	Flower-class corvette	22 August 1940	722	Admiralty
1069	HMS Picotee	Flower-class corvette	5 September 1940	724	Admiralty
1070	HMS Gentian	Flower-class corvette	22 September 1940	723	Admiralty
1071	HMS Hyacinth	Flower-class corvette	3 October 1940	723	Admiralty
1072	HMS Rhododendron	Flower-class corvette	18 October 1940	724	Admiralty
1073	HMS Heather	Flower-class corvette	1 November 1940	724	Admiralty
1074	HMS Freesia	Flower-class corvette	19 November 1940	724	Admiralty
1075	HMS Orchis	Flower-class corvette	29 November 1940	724	Admiralty
1076	HMS Kingcup	Flower-class corvette	3 January 1941	724	Admiralty

No.	Name	Type	Date Completed	Tonnage	Owner
1077	HMS Pimpernel	Flower-class corvette	9 January 1941	724	Admiralty
1078	Dindsdale	Oil tanker	11 April 1942	8,214	Ministry of Shipping
1079	Empire Spenser	Oil tanker	29 April 1942	8,194	Ministry of Shipping
1080	Empire Chapman	Oil tanker	25 June 1942	8,194	Ministry of Shipping
1081	Empire Fletcher	Oil tanker	31 July 1942	8,194	Ministry of Shipping
1082	Deseado	Refrigerated cargo ship	28 November 1942	9,641	Royal Mail
1083	Empire Onyx	Oil tanker	25 December 1941	8,220	Ministry of Shipping
1084	HMS Romeo	Trawler	28 June 1941	545	Admiralty
1085	HMS Rosalind	Trawler	20 October 1941	545	
1086	HMS Oxlip	Flower-class corvette	27 December 1941	724	Admiralty
1087	HMS Pennywort	Flower-class corvette	5 March 1942	724	Admiralty
1088	Empire Gat	Coaster	2 April 1941	871	Ministry of Shipping
1089	Empire Spinney	Coaster	23 September 1941	871	Ministry of Shipping
1090	San Veronico	Oil tanker	31 December 1942	8,189	Eagle Oil Co.
1091	HMS Campania	Aircraft carrier	7 March 1944	12,450	Admiralty
1092	Empire Shoal	Coaster	17 June 1941	878	Ministry of Shipping
1093	Belgian Airman	Cargo ship	25 February 1942	6,960	Ministry of Shipping
1094	Empire Bede	Cargo ship	31 March 1942	6,959	Ministry of Shipping
1095	HMS Abelia	Flower-class corvette	3 February 1941	724	Admiralty
1096	HMS Alisma	Flower-class corvette	13 February 1941	724	Admiralty
1097	HMS Anchusa	Flower-class corvette	1 March 1941	808	Admiralty
1098	HMS Armeria	Flower-class corvette	28 March 1941	808	Admiralty
1099	HMS Aster	Flower-class corvette	11 April 1941	808	Admiralty
1100	HMS Bergamot	Flower-class corvette	9 May 1941	808	Admiralty
1101	HMS Vervain	Flower-class corvette	9 June 1941	808	Admiralty
1102	HMS Bryony	Flower-class corvette	16 June 1942	808	Admiralty
1103	HMS Buttercup	Flower-class corvette	24 April 1942	808	Admiralty

No.	Name	Type	Date Completed	Tonnage	Owner
1104	HMS Chrysanthemum	Flower-class corvette	26 January 1942	808	Admiralty
1105	HMS Cowslip	Flower-class corvette	9 August 1941	811	Admiralty
1106	HMS Eglantine	Flower-class corvette	27 August 1941	811	Admiralty
1107	HMS Fritillary	Flower-class corvette	31 October 1941	811	Admiralty
1108	HMS Genista	Flower-class corvette	18 December 1941	811	Admiralty
1109	Cancelled	Flower-class corvette			Admiralty
1110	Cancelled	Flower-class corvette			Admiralty
1111	Cancelled	Flower-class corvette			Admiralty
1112	Cancelled	Flower-class corvette			Admiralty
1113	Cancelled	Flower-class corvette			Admiralty
1114	Cancelled	Flower-class corvette			Admiralty
1115	Empire Deep	Coaster	30 October 1941	878	Ministry of Shipping
1116	Empire Vigilance	Oil tanker	23 May 1942	8,093	Ministry of Shipping
1117	British Merit	Oil tanker	9 July 1942	8,093	British Tanker Co.
1118	Empire Sidney	Cargo ship	7 May 1942	6,946	Ministry of Shipping
1119	Empire Splendour	Cargo ship	1 September 1942	7,335	Ministry of Shipping
1120	Empire Strength	Cargo ship	22 December 1942	7,355	Ministry of Shipping
1121	TLC 1	Tank landing craft	16 December 1940	229	Admiralty
1122	TLC 2	Tank landing craft	16 December 1940	229	Admiralty
1123	HMS Stronsay	Trawler	24 April 1942	545	Admiralty
1124	HMS Switha	Trawler	15 June 1942	545	Admiralty
1125	Empire castle	Cargo ship	31 January 1943	7,356	Ministry of Shipping
1126	TLC 25	Tank landing craft	25 March 1941	229	Admiralty
1127	TLC 26	Tank landing craft	25 March 1941	229	Admiralty
1128	TLC 100	Tank landing craft	29 June 1941	258	Admiralty
1129	TLC 101	Tank landing craft	11 July 1941	258	Admiralty

No.	Name	Type	Date Completed	Tonnage	Owner
1130	TLC 102	Tank landing craft	31 August 1941	258	Admiralty
1131	TLC 103	Tank landing craft	16 September 1941	258	Admiralty
1132	HMS Algerine	Algerine-class minesweeper	24 March 1942	1,054	Admiralty
1133	HMS Alarm	Algerine-class minesweeper	16 May 1942	1,054	Admiralty
1134	HMS Albacore	Algerine-class minesweeper	16 June 1942	1,054	Admiralty
1135	HMS Acute	Algerine-class minesweeper	30 July 1942	1,054	Admiralty
1136	HMS Cadmus	Algerine-class minesweeper	9 September 1942	1,054	Admiralty
1137	HMS Circe	Algerine-class minesweeper	16 October 1942	1,053	Admiralty
1138	HMS Espiegle	Algerine-class minesweeper	1 December 1942	1,053	Admiralty
1139	HMS Fantome	Algerine-class minesweeper	22 January 1943	1,053	Admiralty
1140	HMS Mutine	Algerine-class minesweeper	26 February 1943	1,053	Admiralty
1141	HMS Onyx	Algerine-class minesweeper	26 March 1943	1,053	Admiralty
1142	HMS Rattler	Algerine-class minesweeper	22 April 1943	1,053	Admiralty
1143	HMS Ready	Algerine-class minesweeper	21 May 1943	1,053	Admiralty
1144	HMS Rinaldo	Algerine-class minesweeper	18 June 1943	1,053	Admiralty
1145	HMS Rosario	Algerine-class minesweeper	9 July 1943	1,053	Admiralty
1146	HMS Spanker	Algerine-class minesweeper	20 August 1943	1,053	Admiralty
1147	HMS Vestal	Algerine-class minesweeper	10 September 1943	1,053	Admiralty
1148	Darro	Refrigerated cargo ship	29 June 1943	9,733	Royal Mail
1149	Pampas	Cargo ship	1 February 1944	8,244	Royal Mail
1150	Rowallan Castle	Refrigerated cargo ship	23 April 1943	7,950	Union Castle
1151	Empire Maiden	Oil tanker	10 March 1942	613	Ministry of Shipping
1152	Paraguay	Cargo ship	7 September 1944	5,560	Royal Mail
1153	HMS Thruster	Tank landing craft	14 March 1943	5,593	Admiralty
1154	HMS Bruiser	Tank landing craft	2 April 1943	5,596	Admiralty
1155	HMS Boxer	Tank landing craft	1 May 1943	5,596	Admiralty

No.	Name	Type	Date Completed	Tonnage	Owner
1156	Samanco	Cargo ship	9 August 1943	8,336	PSNC
1157	Sarmiento	Cargo ship	28 October 1943	8,335	PSNC
1158	Empire Bombardier	Oil tanker	18 February 1943	8,202	Ministry of Shipping
1159	Empire Industry	Oil tanker	16 September 1943	8,203	Ministry of Shipping
1160	Empire Metal	Oil tanker	24 September 1942	8,201	Ministry of Shipping
1161	Waiwera	Refrigerated cargo ship	29 October 1944	12,028	Shaw Savill
1162	HMS Kale	River-class corvette	4 December 1942	1,370	Admiralty
1163	San Vulfrano	Oil tanker	30 December 1942	8,167	Eagle Oil Co.
1164	Empire Benefit	Oil tanker	20 April 1943	8,202	Ministry of Shipping
1165	Empire Grange	Cargo ship	17 March 1943	6,981	Ministry of Shipping
1166	British Patience	Oil tanker	15 June 1943	8,097	British Tanker Co.
1167	Empire MacKay	Aircraft carrier (merchant)	5 October 1943	8,908	Admiralty
1168	Empire Torrent	Cargo ship	29 December 1942	7,076	Ministry of Shipping
1169	Empire Nerissa	Cargo ship	23 February 1943	7,076	Ministry of Shipping
1170	HMS Tweed	River-class corvette	28 April 1943	1,370	Admiralty
1171	HMCS Ontario	Cruiser	25 May 1945	8,800	Royal Canadian Navy
1172	HMS Oxna	Trawler	22 May 1943	545	Admiralty
1173	Narica	Oil tanker	28 May 1943	8,213	Anglo Saxon Petroleum Co.
1174	Neritina	Oil tanker	3 December 1943	8,228	Anglo Saxon Petroleum Co.
1175	Empire Gypsy	Oil tanker	11 November 1942	813	Ministry of Shipping
1176	Drina	Refrigerated cargo ship	25 July 1944	9,787	Royal Mail
1177	Durango	Refrigerated cargo ship	20 December 1944	9,806	Royal Mail
1178	Richmond Castle	Refrigerated cargo ship	28 September 1944	7,971	Union Castle
1179	Cancelled				Blue Star Line
1180	Cancelled				Blue Star Line
1181	Devis	Cargo ship	20 August 1944	8,187	Lamport & Holt
1182	Defoe	Cargo ship	31 May 1945	8,472	Lamport & Holt
1183	San Vito	Oil tanker	30 December 1943	8,164	Eagle Oil Co.
1184	Empire Fay	Oil tanker	21 April 1943	814	Ministry of Shipping

No.	Name	Type	Date Completed	Tonnage	Owner
1185	HMS Helmsdale	River-class corvette	15 October 1943	1,370	Admiralty
1186	HMS Meon	River-class corvette	31 December 1943	1,460	Admiralty
1187	Roxburgh Castle	Refrigerated cargo ship	14 February 1945	8,003	Union Castle
1188	Port Hobart	Refrigerated cargo ship	29 August 1946	11,149	Port Line Ltd
1189	Empire Traveller	Oil tanker	28 October 1943	8,201	Ministry of Shipping
1190	Empire Coppice	Oil tanker	22 June 1943	814	Ministry of Shipping
1191	HMS Glory	Colossus-class aircraft carrier	2 April 1945	13,190	Admiralty
1192	Santander	Cargo ship	2 May 1946	6,612	PSNC
1193	Salaverry	Cargo ship	16 August 1946	6,612	PSNC
1194	Norrisia	Oil tanker	3 March 1944	8,246	Anglo Saxon Petroleum Co.
1195	Nassarius	Oil tanker	30 March 1944	8,246	Anglo Saxon Petroleum Co.
1196	British Might	Oil tanker	7 June 1945	8,289	British Tanker Co.
1197	British Piper	Oil tanker	11 April 1946	8,289	British Tanker Co.
1198	Niso	Oil tanker	20 December 1944	8,273	Anglo Saxon Petroleum Co.
1199	Newcombia	Oil tanker	22 March 1945	8,292	Anglo Saxon Petroleum Co.
1200	Parma	Cargo ship	8 July 1944	5,596	Royal Mail
1201	HMS Pickle	Algerine-class minesweeper	15 October 1943	1,083	Admiralty
1202	HMS Pincher	Algerine-class minesweeper	12 November 1943	1,084	Admiralty
1203	HMS Plucky	Algerine-class minesweeper	10 December 1943	1,084	Admiralty
1204	HMS Recruit	Algerine-class minesweeper	14 January 1944	1,084	Admiralty
1205	HMS Rifleman	Algerine-class minesweeper	11 February 1944	1,084	Admiralty
1206	HMS Squirrel	Algerine-class minesweeper	16 August 1944	1,084	Admiralty
1207	HMS Chameleon	Algerine-class minesweeper	14 September 1944	1,084	Admiralty
1208	HMS Cheerful	Algerine-class minesweeper	13 October 1944	1,084	Admiralty
1209	HMS Hare	Algerine-class minesweeper	10 November 1944	1,084	Admiralty
1210	HMS Jewel	Algerine-class minesweeper	9 December 1944	1,084	Admiralty
1211	HMS Liberty	Algerine-class minesweeper	18 January 1945	1,084	Admiralty

No.	Name	Type	Date Completed	Tonnage	Owner
1212	Cancelled	Algerine-class minesweeper			Admiralty
1213	Cancelled	Algerine-class minesweeper			Admiralty
1214	Cancelled	Algerine-class minesweeper			Admiralty
1215	Cancelled	Algerine-class minesweeper			Admiralty
1216	Cancelled	Algerine-class minesweeper			Admiralty
1217	Cancelled	Algerine-class minesweeper			Admiralty
1218	Cancelled	Algerine-class minesweeper			Admiralty
1219	Empire Outpost	Cargo ship	31 May 1943	6,978	Ministry of Shipping
1220	HMS Eagle	Aircraft carrier	31 October 1951	36,800	Admiralty
1221	HMCS Long Branch	Flower-class corvette	15 January 1944	960	Royal Canadian Navy
1222	Wave King	Oil tanker	22 July 1944	8,159	Admiralty
1223	Wave Monarch	Oil tanker	3 November 1944	8,158	Admiralty
1224	HMS Warrior	Aircraft carrier	14 March 1946	13,350	Admiralty
1225	Empire Harvest	Oil tanker	30 December 1943	814	Ministry of Shipping
1226	HMS Halladale	River-class corvette	11 May 1944	1,370	Admiralty
1227	Empire Dombey	Oil tanker	26 June 1944	813	Ministry of Shipping
1228	HMS Magnificent	Aircraft carrier	21 May 1948	14,000	Admiralty
1229	HMCS Bonaventure	Aircraft carrier	21 January 1957	14,000	Royal Canadian Navy
1230	Empire Abercorn	Refrigerated cargo ship	30 June 1945	8,564	Ministry of Shipping
1231	Empire Clarendon	Refrigerated cargo ship	26 October 1945	8,577	Ministry of Shipping
1232	Cancelled				
1233	Cancelled				
1234	Empire Rangoon	Cargo ship	30 May 1944	6,988	Ministry of Shipping
1235	HMS Humberstone	Castle-class corvette	20 September 1944	1,100	Admiralty
1236	HMS Oakham Castle	Castle-class corvette	10 December 1944	1,100	Admiralty
1237	Cancelled	Castle-class corvette			Admiralty
1238	HMS Oxford Castle	Castle-class corvette	10 March 1944	1,100	Admiralty
1239	HMS Pevensey Castle	Castle-class corvette	10 June 1944	1,100	Admiralty

No.	Name	Type	Date Completed	Tonnage	Owner
1240	HMS Rising Castle	Castle-class corvette	26 June 1944	1,100	Admiralty
1241	HMS Sherborne Castle	Castle-class corvette	14 July 1944	1,100	Admiralty
1242	Empire Saturn	Oil tanker	20 September 1944	8,217	Ministry of Shipping
1243	Empire Jupiter	Oil tanker	29 December 1944	8,217	Ministry of Shipping
1244	Cancelled	Castle-class corvette			Admiralty
1245	Cancelled	Castle-class corvette			Admiralty
1246	HMS Loch Craggie	Loch-class frigate	15 June 1944	1,435	Admiralty
1247	HMS Loch Gorm	Loch-class frigate	7 July 1944	1,435	Admiralty
1248	HMS Loch Killisport	Loch-class frigate	9 September 1945	1,435	Admiralty
1249	HMS St Austell Bay	Bay-class frigate	29 May 1945	1,600	Admiralty
1250	HMS St Brides Bay	Bay-class frigate	15 June 1945	1,600	Admiralty
1251	SAS Transvaal	Loch-class frigate	2 January 1945	1,435	South African Navy
1252	HMS Start Bay	Bay-class frigate	6 September 1945	1,600	Admiralty
1253	HMS Tremadoc Bay	Bay-class frigate	11 October 1945	1,600	Admiralty
1254	Cancelled	Loch-class frigate			Admiralty
1255	Cancelled	Loch-class frigate			Admiralty
1256	Cancelled	Loch-class frigate			Admiralty
1257	Cancelled	Loch-class frigate			Admiralty
1258	Cancelled	Loch-class frigate			Admiralty
1259	HMS Widemouth Bay	Bay-class frigate	13 April 1945	1,600	Admiralty
1260	HMS Wigtown Bay	Bay-class frigate	19 January 1946	1,600	Admiralty
1261	HMS Whitesand Bay	Bay-class frigate	30 July 1945	1,600	Admiralty
1262	Cancelled	Loch-class frigate			Admiralty
1263	Cancelled	Loch-class frigate			Admiralty
1264	Cancelled	Loch-class frigate			Admiralty
1265	Cancelled	Loch-class frigate			Admiralty
1266	Cancelled	Loch-class frigate			Admiralty
1267	Cancelled	Loch-class frigate			Admiralty
1268	Cancelled	Loch-class frigate			Admiralty
1269	Cancelled	Loch-class frigate			Admiralty
1270	Cancelled	Loch-class frigate			Admiralty

No.	Name	Type	Date Completed	Tonnage	Owner
1271	Cancelled	Loch-class frigate			Admiralty
1272	Cancelled	Loch-class frigate			Admiralty
1273	Cancelled	Loch-class frigate			Admiralty
1274	Cancelled	Loch-class frigate			Admiralty
1275	Cancelled	Loch-class frigate			Admiralty
1276	Empire Falkland	Cargo ship	21 February 1945	7,006	Ministry of Shipping
1277	Riebeeck Castle	Refrigerated cargo ship	11 March 1946	22,000	Union Castle
1278	Rustenburg Castle	Refrigerated cargo ship	25 June 1946	23,300	Union Castle
1279	Pilcomayo	Cargo ship	14 December 1945	5,567	Royal Mail
1280	HMS Hermes	Aircraft carrier	22 September 1953	22,000	Admiralty
1281	HMS Bulwark	Aircraft carrier	2 November 1953	22,000	Admiralty
1282	Empire Jura	Oil tanker	16 October 1944	813	Ministry of Shipping
1283	Empire Gambia	Cargo ship	10 July 1945	7,058	Ministry of Shipping
1284	British Supremacy	Oil tanker	21 December 1945	8,242	British Tanker Co.
1285	Neothyris	Oil tanker	24 January 1946	8,243	Anglo Saxon Petroleum Co.
1286	Empire Bute	Oil tanker	22 December 1944	812	Ministry of Shipping
1287	Empire Orkney	Oil tanker	26 February 1945	812	Ministry of Shipping
1288	Empire Shetland	Oil tanker	11 April 1945	812	Ministry of Shipping
1289	TF 6	Landing ship	15 September 1944	4,157	Admiralty
1290	TF 7	Landing ship	28 September 1944	4,157	Admiralty
1291	TF 8	Landing ship	4 May 1945	4,157	Admiralty
1292	TF 9	Landing ship	11 May 1945	4,157	Admiralty
1293	TF 10	Landing ship	5 April 1945	4,157	Admiralty
1294	TF 11	Landing ship	14 August 1945	4,157	Admiralty
1295	TF 12	Landing ship	25 September 1945	4,157	Admiralty
1296	TF 13	Landing ship	24 November 1945	4,157	Admiralty
1297	TF 41	Landing ship	6 June 1945	4,157	Admiralty
1298	TF 42	Landing ship	16 November 1945	4,157	Admiralty
1299	Empire Belgrave	Oil tanker	19 June 1945	890	Ministry of Shipping
1300	Empire Campden	Oil tanker	14 August 1945	890	Ministry of Shipping
1301	Empire Fitzroy	Oil tanker	9 October 1945	890	Ministry of Shipping
1302	Empire Grosvenor	Oil tanker	27 November 1945	890	Ministry of Shipping

No.	Name	Type	Date Completed	Tonnage	Owner
1303	Empire Star	Cargo ship	18 December 1946	11,860	Blue Star Line
1304	Cancelled				
1305	Cancelled				
1306	Wave Chief	Oil tanker	27 August 1946	8,097	Admiralty
1307	British Knight	Oil tanker	25 September 1946	8,629	British Tanker Co.
1308	Lyria	Oil tanker	20 June 1946	6,452	Anglo Saxon Petroleum Co.
1309	Linga	Oil tanker	19 September 1946	6,452	Anglo Saxon Petroleum Co.
1310	Calchas	Cargo ship	17 January 1947	8,298	Alfred Holt
1311	Empire Tedship	Oil tanker	4 February 1946	890	Ministry of Shipping
1312	Empire Tedport	Oil tanker	12 March 1945	890	Ministry of Shipping
1313	Empire Tedmuir	Oil tanker	7 May 1946	890	Ministry of Shipping
1314	Empire Tedrita	Oil tanker	6 September 1946	890	Ministry of Shipping
1315	Empire Tesland	Oil tanker	19 September 1945	979	Ministry of Shipping
1316	Patella	Bitumen tanker	17 December 1946	8,277	Anglo Saxon Petroleum Co.
1317	Empire Tedscombe	Oil tanker	24 December 1945	980	Ministry of Shipping
1318	Empire Tessella	Oil tanker	7 February 1946	980	Ministry of Shipping
1319	Cancelled				Ministry of Shipping
1320	Cancelled				Ministry of Shipping
1321	Cancelled				Ministry of Shipping
1322	Cancelled				Ministry of Shipping
1323	Cancelled				Ministry of Shipping
1324	Cancelled				Ministry of Shipping
1325	TF 40	Landing ship	26 January 1946	4,273	Admiralty
1326	Athenic	Passenger ship	16 July 1947	15,187	Shaw Savill
1327	Balena	Whale factory ship	28 September 1946	15,715	United Whalers Ltd
1328	Loch Garth	Refrigerated cargo ship	29 May 1947	8,617	Royal Mail
1329	Loch Avon	Refrigerated cargo ship	3 September 1947	8,617	Royal Mail
1330	Waverley	Paddle steamer	5 June 1947	693	London & North Eastern Railway

No.	Name	Type	Date Completed	Tonnage	Owner
1331	Parthia	Passenger ship	7 April 1948	13,362	Cunard-White Star Line
1332	Pretoria Castle	Passenger ship	10 July 1948	28,705	Union Castle
1333	Edinburgh Castle	Passenger ship	26 November 1948	28,705	Union Castle
1334	Linswe	Tug	2 August 1946	20	Ministry of Shipping
1335	Linwet	Tug	2 August 1946	20	Ministry of Shipping
1336	Linyon	Tug	2 August 1946	20	Ministry of Shipping
1337	Linno	Tug	2 August 1946	20	Ministry of Shipping
1338	Linda	Tug	18 September 1946	20	Ministry of Shipping
1339	Limpya	Tug	17 August 1946	20	Ministry of Shipping
1340	Unnamed	Launch	7 October 1946	20	Ministry of Shipping
1341	Unnamed	Launch	28 January 1946	20	Ministry of Shipping
1342	Unnamed	Launch	28 January 1946	20	Ministry of Shipping
1343	La Hague	Cargo ship	4 June 1947	4,027	French Line
1344	Morbihan	Cargo ship	3 July 1947	4,025	French Line
1345	La Heve	Cargo ship	17 September 1947	4,027	French Line
1346	Lepton	Oil tanker	6 February 1947	6,446	Anglo Saxon Petroleum Co.
1347	Lingula	Oil tanker	25 March 1947	6,447	Anglo Saxon Petroleum Co.
1348	Thorshavet	Whale factory ship	9 October 1947	17,081	A/S Thor Dahl Ltd
1349	Munster	Ferry	17 January 1948	4,088	Coast Lines Ltd
1350	Imperial Star	Refrigerated cargo ship	12 March 1948	13,181	Blue Star Line
1351	Melbourne Star	Refrigerated cargo ship	14 July 1948	13,179	Blue Star Line
1352	Leinster	Ferry	25 March 1948	4,115	Coast Lines Ltd
1353	Soochow	Ferry	18 December 1947	2,950	China Navigation Co.
1354	Magdalena	Passenger ship	18 February 1949	17,547	Royal Mail
1355	Pelorus	Pilot boat	28 January 1948	443	Trinity House
1356	Penlee	Pilot boat	7 April 1948	443	Trinity House
1357	Salinas	Cargo ship	18 November 1947	6,669	PSNC
1358	Salamanca	Cargo ship	20 March 1948	6,669	PSNC
1359	Kantara	Cargo ship	19 November 1947	3,213	Moss Hutchinson & Co.

No.	Name	Type	Date Completed	Tonnage	Owner
1360	Karnak	Cargo ship	30 January 1948	3,198	Moss Hutchinson & Co.
1361	Granuaile	Lightship tender	18 July 1948	1,101	Commissioners of Irish Lights
1362	British Ranger	Oil tanker	3 June 1948	8,575	British Tanker Co.
1363	Soestdyk	Cargo ship	14 October 1948	9,582	Holland-America Line
1364	British Security	Oil tanker	7 July 1948	8,583	British Tanker Co.
1365	British Strength	Oil tanker	12 November 1948	8,580	British Tanker Co.
1366	Schiedyk	Cargo ship	19 February 1949	9,582	Holland-America Line
1367	Hibernia	Ferry	5 April 1949	4,972	British Railways
1368	Cambria	Ferry	17 May 1949	4,972	British Railways
1369	Liparus	Oil tanker	7 September 1948	6,473	Anglo Saxon Petroleum Co.
1370	Lotorium	Oil tanker	30 December 1947	6,490	Anglo Saxon Petroleum Co.
1371	Ramore Head	Cargo ship	26 August 1948	6,195	Ulster Steamship Co.
1372	Antilochus	Cargo ship	3 May 1949	8,238	Alfred Holt
1373	Jalta	Oil tanker	17 September 1948	8,247	A/S Bulls Rederi
1374	Saravasti	Ferry	20 June 1949	3,750	Bombay Steam Navigation Co.
1375	Sabaramati	Ferry	20 August 1949	3,750	Bombay Steam Navigation Co.
1376	Helenus	Cargo ship	29 October 1949	10,215	Alfred Holt
1377	Hector	Cargo ship	31 March 1950	10,215	Alfred Holt
1378	British Mariner	Oil tanker	29 December 1948	8,576	British Tanker Co.
1379	British Workman	Oil tanker	24 March 1949	8,575	British Tanker Co.
1380	Borgny	Oil tanker	31 March 1949	8,255	Fred Olsen & Co.
1381	Vestfoss	Oil tanker	27 June 1949	8,250	A/S Thor Thorsen
1382	Explorador	Oil tanker	6 July 1949	6,498	Estrella Maritima S.A.
1383	Vikingen	Oil tanker	7 October 1949	8,263	Panama City Tanker Co.
1384	Juan Peron	Whale factory ship	15 October 1951	25,469	Compañia Argentina de Pesca
1385	Amarna	Cargo ship	6 July 1949	3,422	Moss Hutchinson & Co.
1386	Assiout	Cargo ship	12 October 1949	3,422	Moss Hutchinson & Co.
1387	Champravati	Ferry	20 October 1949	1,288	Bombay Steam Navigation Co.
1388	Rohidas	Ferry	20 October 1949	1,288	Bombay Steam Navigation Co.

No.	Name	Type	Date Completed	Tonnage	Owner
1389	Cazador	Oil tanker	15 June 1949	6,441	Estrella Maritima S.A.
1390	Setter 1	Whale catcher	20 October 1948	599	United Whalers Ltd
1391	Setter 2	Whale catcher	8 November 1948	599	United Whalers Ltd
1392	Ternoy	Oil tanker	27 January 1950	8,218	A/S Truma
1393	Setter 3	Whale catcher	18 August 1949	586	United Whalers Ltd
1394	Setter 4	Whale catcher	2 September 1949	586	United Whalers Ltd
1395	Setter 5	Whale catcher	19 September 1949	586	United Whalers Ltd
1396	Setter 6	Whale catcher	12 October 1947	586	United Whalers Ltd
1397	British Captain	Oil tanker	25 November 1949	8,700	British Tanker Co.
1398	British Commander	Oil tanker	23 February 1950	8,700	British Tanker Co.
1399	British Consul	Oil tanker	9 June 1950	8,700	British Tanker Co.
1400	British Explorer	Oil tanker	8 July 1950	8,700	British Tanker Co.
1401	British Prospector	Oil tanker	28 September 1950	8,700	British Tanker Co.
1402	British Surveyor	Oil tanker	8 December 1950	8,700	British Tanker Co.

Completed Shell Oil tanker *Verena* departs Belfast.

No.	Name	Type	Date Completed	Tonnage	Owner
1403	Verena	Oil tanker	9 November 1950	18,612	Anglo Saxon Petroleum Co.
1404	Bratsberg	Oil tanker	5 October 1950	8,255	Borgestad A/S
1405	Binta	Oil tanker	19 December 1950	8,162	Per Gjerding
1406	Bolette	Oil tanker	17 January 1951	16,394	Fred Olsen & Co.
1407	Dalfonn	Oil tanker	15 May 1951	16,440	Sigval Bergsen
1408	Kurdistan	Oil tanker	24 February 1950	8,322	Commons Bros Ltd
1409	Africana 2	Trawler	27 January 1950	882	South African Government
1410	Tank King	Oil tanker	31 August 1951	16,477	Sigurd Herlofsen A/S
1411	France Stove	Oil tanker	12 November 1951	16,468	Lorentzen A/S
1412	Orkdal	Oil tanker	17 April 1951	8,221	Moltzaua & Christensen
1413	Ringerd	Oil tanker	12 March 1951	8,218	Olav Ringdal
1414	Runic	Refrigerated cargo ship	24 March 1950	13,587	Shaw Savill
1415	Suevic	Refrigerated cargo ship	5 July 1950	13,587	Shaw Savill
1416	Ascanius	Cargo ship	21 November 1950	7,692	Alfred Holt
1417	Ixion	Cargo ship	5 January 1951	10,125	Alfred Holt
1418	Laganfield	Oil tanker	29 December 1950	8,196	Hunting & Sons
1419	Bollsta	Oil tanker	6 October 1951	16,405	Fred Olsen & Co.
1420	Cancelled				
1421	Bloemfontein Castle	Passenger ship	25 March 1950	18,400	Union Castle
1422	Ernst Larsen	Whale catcher	4 November 1949	598	United Whaling Co.
1423	Arnt Larsen	Whale catcher	9 November 1949	598	United Whaling Co.
1424	Cancelled				
1425	British Skill	Oil tanker	12 June 1952	18,550	British Tanker Co.
1426	Cancelled				
1427	Cancelled				
1428	Carnarvon	Whale catcher	27 April 1950	598	Australian Whaling Commission
1429	Simba	Tug	8 June 1950	359	East African Railways
1430	Nyati	Tug	15 September 1951	359	East African Railways
1431	Rhodesia Castle	Passenger ship	6 October 1951	17,041	Union Castle
1432	Kenya Castle	Passenger ship	16 February 1952	17,041	Union Castle
1433	Roonagh Head	Cargo ship	20 March 1952	6,153	Ulster Steamship Co.

No.	Name	Type	Date Completed	Tonnage	Owner
1434	Kvint	Whale catcher	27 November 1950	591	Falkland Shipowners Co.
1435	La Rochelle	Oil tanker	25 April 1952	12,081	Société Navale Delmas Vieljeux
1436	Clydefield	Oil tanker	21 January 1953	11,163	Hunting & Sons
1437	Port Nelson	Cargo ship	31 October 1951	8,375	Port Line Ltd
1438	Eastern Star	Cargo ship	20 December 1951	6,523	Australia China Line
1439	Setter 7	Whale catcher	14 September 1951	588	United Whalers
1440	Setter 8	Whale catcher	11 October 1951	588	United Whalers
1441	Star 9	Whale catcher	30 October 1951	588	Hvalfinger A/S
1442	Ebro	Cargo ship	12 June 1952	5,855	Royal Mail
1443	Janita	Oil tanker	9 July 1952	12,757	Spermacet Whaling Co.
1444	Raeburn	Cargo ship	28 November 1952	8,312	Lamport & Holt
1445	Cedric	Refrigerated cargo ship	11 November 1952	11,232	Shaw Savill
1446	J.K. Hansen	Whale catcher	24 October 1951	742	Union Whaling Co.
1447	Essquibo	Cargo ship	11 September 1952	5,855	Royal Mail
1448	Onitsha	Cargo ship	5 June 1952	5,802	Elder Dempster
1449	Obuassi	Cargo ship	12 November 1952	5,883	Elder Dempster
1450	King Malcolm	Cargo ship	29 February 1952	5,883	King Line
1451	King Alexander	Cargo ship	6 May 1952	5,883	King Line
1452	Janova	Oil tanker	30 January 1953	12,765	Spermacet Whaling Co.
1453	Cymric	Refrigerated cargo ship	15 May 1953	11,182	Shaw Savill
1454	Blandford	Oil tanker	14 May 1953	12,514	Blandford Shipping
1455	Anders Andersen	Whale catcher	15 November 1951	742	Union Whaling Co.
1456	Beaverbank	Cargo ship	26 February 1953	5,690	Andrew Weir
1457	Nessbank	Cargo ship	24 June 1953	5,690	Andrew Weir
1458	Fleetbank	Cargo ship	14 October 1953	5,690	Andrew Weir
1459	Braemar Castle	Passenger ship	8 November 1952	17,029	Union Castle
1460	Irex	Oil tanker	8 July 1953	8,280	A/S Field
1461	Irish Coast	Ferry	17 October 1952	3,824	Coast Lines Ltd
1462	King Arthur	Cargo ship	19 March 1953	5,883	King Line
1463	Britta	Oil tanker	17 September 1953	12,757	Arthur H. Mathiesen
1464	British Engineer	Oil tanker	30 April 1954	21,077	British Tanker Co.
1465	British Corporal	Oil tanker	1 July 1954	10,071	British Tanker Co.
1466	British Gunner	Oil tanker	6 May 1954	10,076	British Tanker Co.

No.	Name	Type	Date Completed	Tonnage	Owner
1467	British Sergeant	Oil tanker	20 August 1954	10,073	British Tanker Co.
1468	Harpa	Oil tanker	11 June 1953	12,202	Anglo Saxon Petroleum Co.
1469	Harvella	Oil tanker	20 September 1956	12,224	Shell Oil Co.
1470	Cerinthus	Oil tanker	9 November 1954	12,194	Hadley Shipping Co.
1471	Jarina	Oil tanker	20 November 1953	12,706	A/S Kosmos
1472	HMS Torquay	Whitby-class frigate	10 May 1956	2,150	Admiralty
1473	HMS Blackpool	Whitby-class frigate	14 August 1958	2,150	Admiralty
1474	Maid of the Loch	Paddle steamer	4 May 1953	555	British Railways
1475	Rathlin Head	Cargo ship	4 November 1953	7,439	Ulster Steamship Co.
1476	Iberia	Passenger ship	10 September 1954	29,614	P&O
1477	Elpenor	Cargo ship	22 April 1954	7,757	Alfred Holt
1478	Jaranda	Oil tanker	9 January 1954	12,776	Anders Jahre A/S
1479	Owerri	Cargo ship	21 January 1955	6,240	Elder Dempster
1480	Loch Gowan	Cargo ship	27 June 1954	9,718	Royal Mail
1481	Cedarbank	Cargo ship	5 January 1955	5,671	Andrew Weir
1482	Port Montreal	Refrigerated cargo ship	4 February 1954	6,843	Port Line Ltd
1483	Port Melbourne	Refrigerated cargo ship	7 July 1955	10,470	Port Line Ltd
1484	Vibex	Oil tanker	20 October 1955	20,787	Shell Oil
1485	Harpula	Oil tanker	21 December 1955	12,258	Shell Oil
1486	Belfast	Oil tanker	24 February 1955	12,744	Belships Company
1487	Cancelled				
1488	HMS Braysford	Seaward defence craft	8 May 1954	110	Admiralty
1489	HMS Bryansford	Seaward defence craft	10 September 1954	110	Admiralty
1490	Cancelled				
1491	Maid of Argyll	Ferry	1 June 1953	508	British Railways
1492	Maid of Skelmorlie	Ferry	24 June 1953	508	British Railways
1493	Solfonn	Oil tanker	13 June 1956	19,810	Sigval Bergsen
1494	Pontia		15 September 1954	8,904	Pelagos A/S
1495	Cancelled				
1496	Triaster	Cargo ship	21 October 1955	9,994	British Phosphate Carriers
1497	Dolius	Cargo ship	5 January 1956	7,964	Alfred Holt
1498	Southern Cross	Passenger ship	28 February 1955	20,204	Shaw Savill
1499	Tantallon Castle	Cargo ship	5 March 1954	7,448	Union Castle

No.	Name	Type	Date Completed	Tonnage	Owner
1500	Tintagel Castle	Cargo ship	5 June 1954	7,447	Union Castle
1501	YC 327	Lighter	1 July 1954	561	Admiralty
1502	RAFA Tide Austral	Fleet tanker	17 May 1955	13,165	Royal Australian Navy
1503	Busen 5	Whale catcher	5 September 1952	588	Tongsberg A/S
1504	Ballylumford	Collier	7 May 1954	1,242	John Kelly Ltd
1505	Cancelled				
1506	Cancelled				
1507	Setter 11	Whale catcher	19 November 1953	739	Hector Whaling Ltd
1508	Western Prince	Cargo ship	27 April 1955	7,917	Prince Line
1509	Rowanmore	Cargo ship	27 June 1956	8,497	Johnston Warren & Co.
1510	Cancelled				
1511	Elin Knudsen	Oil tanker	11 April 1956	20,492	Knut Knudsen A/S
1512	Vitrina	Oil tanker	4 July 1957	20,803	Shell Oil
1513	Southern Prince	Cargo ship	8 March 1956	7,917	Prince Line
1514	Foylebank	Cargo ship	4 August 1955	5,671	Andrew Weir
1515	Laganbank	Cargo ship	27 October 1955	5,671	Andrew Weir
1516	Cancelled				
1517	HMS Kemerton	Ton-class minesweeper	21 May 1954	360	Admiralty
1518	HMS Kirkliston	Ton-class minesweeper	21 August 1954	360	Admiralty
1519	HMS Laleston	Ton-class minesweeper	10 November 1954	360	Admiralty
1520	HMS Lanton	Ton-class minesweeper	10 March 1955	360	Admiralty
1521	HMS Letterston	Ton-class minesweeper	29 June 1955	360	Admiralty
1522	HMS Leverton	Ton-class minesweeper	25 August 1955	360	Admiralty
1523	HMS Kildarton	Ton-class minesweeper	25 November 1955	360	Admiralty
1524	HMS Lullington	Ton-class minesweeper	1 June 1956	360	Admiralty
1525	HMS Maddiston	Ton-class minesweeper	8 November 1956	360	Admiralty
1526	HMS Maxton	Ton-class minesweeper	19 February 1957	360	Admiralty
1527	HMS Nurton	Ton-class minesweeper	21 August 1957	360	Admiralty
1528	HMS Repton	Ton-class minesweeper	11 December 1957	360	Admiralty
1529	HMS Confiance	Tug	19 March 1956	760	Admiralty

No.	Name	Type	Date Completed	Tonnage	Owner
1530	HMS Confident	Tug	6 September 1956	760	Admiralty
1531	British Honour	Oil tanker	31 January 1958	21,031	British Tanker Co.
1532	Cancelled				
1533	Reina del Mar	Passenger ship	8 April 1956	20,225	PSNC
1534	Port Launceston	Refrigerated cargo ship	12 March 1957	8,957	Port Line Ltd
1535	Cancelled				
1536	Cancelled				
1537	Ulster Premier	Coaster	20 September 1955	979	Belfast Steamship Co.
1538	Storfonn	Oil tanker	31 January 1957	24,858	Sigval Bergsen
1539	Escalante	Cargo ship	14 December 1955	7,791	Royal Mail
1540	Duke of Lancaster	Ferry	22 August 1956	4,979	British Railways
1541	Duke of Argyll	Ferry	22 September 1956	4,979	British Railways
1542	Missouri	Oil tanker	26 January 1957	18,751	Texaco Oil Co.
1543	New Mexico	Oil tanker	13 September 1958	18,751	Texaco Oil Co.
1544	Eden	Refrigerated cargo ship	1 February 1956	7,791	Royal Mail
1545	Tuscany	Refrigerated cargo ship	25 October 1956	7,455	Royal Mail
1546	Oti	Cargo ship	26 April 1956	5,485	Elder Dempster
1547	Scottish Coast	Ferry	1 March 1957	3,817	Coast Lines Ltd
1548	Cloverbank	Cargo ship	7 March 1957	6,459	Andrew Weir
1549	Crestbank	Cargo ship	7 June 1957	6,459	Andrew Weir
1550	Carronbank	Cargo ship	27 September 1957	6,461	Andrew Weir
1551	Dartbank	Cargo ship	17 January 1958	6,461	Andrew Weir
1552	Garrybank	Cargo ship	2 April 1958	8,693	Andrew Weir
1553	Minchbank	Cargo ship	25 September 1957	8,693	Andrew Weir
1554	Ondo	Cargo ship	24 October 1956	5,435	Elder Dempster
1555	INS Trishul	Whitby-class frigate	14 January 1960	2,150	Indian Navy
1556	King Charles	Cargo ship	25 June 1957	5,993	King Line
1557	King George	Cargo ship	19 December 1957	5,989	King Line
1558	Pendennis Castle	Passenger ship	14 November 1958	28,582	Union Castle
1559	Albany	Refrigerated cargo ship	13 February 1957	7,299	Royal Mail
1560	Picardy	Refrigerated cargo ship	22 August 1957	7,306	Royal Mail
1561	Thessaly	Refrigerated cargo ship	26 September 1957	7,299	Royal Mail
1562	Loch Loyal	Refrigerated cargo ship	30 December 1957	11,035	Royal Mail
1563	Lappe	Lighter	23 March 1956	165	Shell Oil

No.	Name	Type	Date Completed	Tonnage	Owner
1564	Flying Duck	Tug	29 October 1956	176	Clyde Shipping Co.
1565	Port Invercargill	Refrigerated cargo ship	26 March 1958	8,847	Port Line Ltd
1566	Alaric	Cargo ship	13 February 1958	6,692	Shaw Savill
1567	Afghanistan	Ore carrier	20 June 1957	11,188	Commons Bros Ltd
1568	Ulster Star	Refrigerated cargo ship	3 July 1959	10,413	Blue Star Line
1569	Esso Glasgow	Oil tanker	17 August 1957	10,720	Esso Petroleum Co.
1570	Flying Drake	Tug	17 May 1957	177	Clyde Shipping Co.
1571	Eskfield	Oil tanker	22 December 1959	18,851	Hunting & Sons
1572	British Statesman	Oil tanker	18 April 1959	27,586	British Tanker Co.
1573	British Power	Oil tanker	15 November 1959	27,586	British Tanker Co.
1574	William Wheelwright	Oil tanker	1 July 1960	31,320	PSNC
1575	Edward Stevenson	Oil tanker	27 February 1961	31,317	Stevenson Hardy & Co.
1576	Carrigan Head	Cargo ship	18 November 1958	8,271	Ulster Steamship Co.

The Blue Star refrigerated cargo ship *Ulster Star* fitting out, June 1959.

No.	Name	Type	Date Completed	Tonnage	Owner
1577	Iron Age	Ore carrier	22 May 1958	11,188	Vallum Shipping Co.
1578	Vestfonn	Oil tanker	11 July 1958	13,409	Sigval Bergsen
1579	Accord	Tug	15 October 1958	640	Admiralty
1580	Advice	Tug	17 June 1959	640	Admiralty
1581	Tri-Ellis	Phosphate carrier	31 October 1958	11,760	British Phosphate Carriers
1582	Manchester Miller	Cargo ship	19 March 1959	9,297	Manchester Liners Ltd
1583	SAS Port Elizabeth	Ton-class minesweeper	10 July 1958	360	South African Navy
1584	SAS Mosselbaai	Ton-class minesweeper	11 February 1959	360	South African Navy
1585	SAS Walvisbaai	Ton-class minesweeper	21 May 1959	360	South African Navy
1586	Cancelled				
1587	King Henry	Cargo ship	5 December 1958	6,133	King Line
1588	British Mallard	Oil tanker	6 May 1960	11,174	British Tanker Co.
1589	British Gull	Oil tanker	29 April 1960	11,156	British tanker Co.
1590	HMS Berwick	Rothesay-class frigate	9 June 1961	2,519	Admiralty
1591	HMS Leander	Leander-class frigate	28 March 1963	2,450	Admiralty
1592	Ashbank	Cargo ship	2 May 1959	8,694	Andrew Weir
1593	Rosebank	Cargo ship	3 April 1959	8,693	Andrew Weir
1594	Amazon	Passenger ship	31 December 1959	20,348	Royal Mail
1595	Aragon	Passenger ship	12 April 1960	20,362	Royal Mail
1596	Arlanza	Passenger ship	23 September 1960	20,362	Royal Mail
1597	Tindfonn	Oil tanker	30 May 1961	31,322	Sigval Bergsen
1598	Cancelled				
1599	Tresfonn	Bulk carrier	11 June 1960	13,471	Sigval Bergsen
1600	British Lancer	Oil tanker	28 June 1963	32,547	British Tanker Co.
1601	British Vine	Oil tanker	26 March 1965	13,408	British Tanker Co.
1602	British Centaur	Oil tanker	11 January 1966	37,985	British Tanker Co.
1603	Norsk Drott	Oil tanker	28 April 1961	18,434	Norsk Braendselojle A/S
1604	British Cormorant	Oil tanker	6 July 1961	11,132	British Tanker Co.
1605	British Osprey	Oil tanker	12 January 1962	11,132	British Tanker Co.
1606	British Merlin	Oil tanker	19 May 1962	11,132	British Tanker Co.
1607	British Cygnet	Oil tanker	7 June 1962	11,131	British Tanker Co.
1608	Cancelled				
1609	Bulimba	Cargo ship	26 March 1958	6,796	British India Steam Navigation Co.

Royal Mail ship *Aragon* outfitting, while *Chusan* undergoes repairs.

No.	Name	Type	Date Completed	Tonnage	Owner
1610	Bankura	Cargo ship	27 August 1959	6,793	British India Steam Navigation Co.
1611	Barpeta	Cargo ship	19 September 1960	6,736	British India Steam Navigation Co.
1612	Bamora	Cargo ship	30 January 1961	6,744	British India Steam Navigation Co.
1613	Bombala	Cargo ship	28 August 1961	6,744	British India Steam Navigation Co.
1614	Regent Liverpool	Oil tanker	23 November 1962	30,770	Texaco Oil Co.
1615	Flying Dipper	Tug	27 March 1958	274	Clyde Shipping Co.
1616	Cancelled				
1617	Cancelled				
1618	Cancelled				
1619	Krossfon	Bulk carrier	8 April 1961	13,481	Sigval Bergsen
1620	Rimfonn	Oil tanker	18 December 1963	50,677	Sigval Bergsen
1621	Canberra	Passenger ship	19 May 1961	45,270	P&O
1622	Somers Isle	Cargo ship	10 July 1959	5,684	PSNC
1623	Wakefield	Coaster	8 October 1958	1,113	Associated Humber Lines

No.	Name	Type	Date Completed	Tonnage	Owner
1624	Leeds	Coaster	16 April 1959	1,113	Associated Humber Lines
1625	York	Coaster	14 November 1959	1,113	Associated Humber Lines
1626	George Peacock	Oil tanker	6 July 1961	18,863	PSNC
1627	Cancelled				
1628	Cancelled				
1629	Cancelled				
1630	Port Alfred	Refrigerated cargo ship	1 March 1961	9,044	Port Line Ltd
1631	Port St Lawrence	Refrigerated cargo ship	20 October 1961	9,040	Port Line Ltd
1632	HMS Kent	County-class destroyer	17 August 1963	5,200	Admiralty
1633	Icenic	Refrigerated cargo ship	19 December 1960	11,239	Shaw Savill
1634	Cancelled				
1635	Pinebank	Cargo ship	24 September 1959	8,694	Andrew Weir
1636	Elmbank	Cargo ship	28 April 1960	8,694	Andrew Weir
1637	Avonbank	Cargo ship	13 January 1961	8,694	Andrew Weir
1638	Levernbank	Cargo ship	11 August 1961	8,694	Andrew Weir
1639	Springbank	Cargo ship	26 January 1962	8,694	Andrew Weir
1640	Olivebank	Cargo ship	12 April 1962	8,694	Andrew Weir
1641	Cancelled				
1642	Daghestan	Ore carrier	1 November 1960	11,210	Hindustan Shipping Co.
1643	Clyde	Launch	13 March 1961	65	Clyde Navigation Trust
1644	Cressington	Dredger	4 April 1962	1,431	British Transport Commission
1645	Aigburth	Dredger	29 March 1963	1,037	British Transport Commission
1646	Port Nicholson	Refrigerated cargo ship	9 November 1962	13,847	Port Line Ltd
1647	Roybank	Cargo ship	31 October 1963	6,526	Andrew Weir
1648	Weybank	Cargo ship	26 March 1964	6,527	Andrew Weir
1649	Ringwood	Cargo ship	29 September 1962	10,860	Ringals Rederi A/S
1650	Bellisland	Cargo ship	23 January 1963	10,862	Belships Co.
1651	HMS Fearless	Assault ship	27 November 1965	11,060	Admiralty
1652	Lossibank	Cargo ship	3 July 1963	8,678	Andrew Weir
1653	Methane Progress	LNG carrier	26 May 1964	21,875	Methane Tanker Finance Co.
1654	Hazelbank	Cargo ship	20 May 1964	10,507	Andrew Weir
1655	Irisbank	Cargo ship	9 September 1964	10,507	Andrew Weir

No.	Name	Type	Date Completed	Tonnage	Owner
1656	Texaco Maracaibo	Oil tanker	14 January 1965	51,774	Texaco Oil Co.
1657	HMNZS Waikato	Leander-class frigate	19 September 1966	2,305	Royal New Zealand Navy
1658	RFA Regent	Fleet oiler	6 June 1967	19,000	Admiralty
1659	Edenfield	Oil tanker	2 July 1967	35,805	Eden Tankers Ltd
1660	La Estancia	Bulk carrier	30 September 1965	28,007	Buries Marks Ltd
1661	La Sierra	Bulk carrier	12 February 1966	28,004	Buries Marks Ltd
1662	Orcoma	Oil tanker	30 March 1966	10,509	Shell International Marine
1663	Donax	Oil tanker	16 December 1966	42,068	Shell International Marine
1664	Cancelled				
1665	Nairnbank	Cargo ship	7 July 1966	10,541	Andrew Weir
1666	Myrina	Oil tanker	24 April 1968	95,450	Deutsche Shell AG
1667	Ulster Prince	Ferry	6 April 1967	4,478	Coast Lines Ltd
1668	Fjordaas	Bulk carrier	29 August 1967	41,079	Norwegian Bulk Carriers Ltd
1669	Essi Kristine	Bulk carrier	1 March 1968	41,079	Norwegian Bulk Carriers Ltd
1670	Skaufast	Bulk carrier	29 October 1968	57,204	Norwegian Bulk Carriers Ltd
1671	Thara	Bulk carrier	28 August 1968	41,089	Norwegian Bulk Carriers Ltd
1672	Aino	Bulk carrier	16 May 1969	57,204	C.H. Sorensen
1673	Maplebank	Cargo ship	15 August 1967	10,365	Andrew Weir
1674	Gowanbank	Cargo ship	30 January 1968	10,365	Andrew Weir
1675	HMS Charybdis	Leander-class frigate	6 June 1969	2,450	Admiralty
1676	Esso Ulidia	Oil tanker	6 October 1970	126,538	Esso Petroleum Co.
1677	Esso Caledonia	Oil tanker	6 September 1971	126,535	Esso Petroleum Co.
1678	La Pampa	Bulk carrier	13 May 1970	17,180	Buries Marks Ltd
1679	Bulk Eagle	Bulk carrier	14 September 1970	17,180	Kriship Shipping Co.
1680	Sydney Bridge	Bulk carrier	10 September 1970	35,868	Bowring Shipping Ltd
1681	Cancelled				
1682	Cancelled				
1683	Cancelled				
1684	Rudby	Bulk carrier	1 March 1971	57,245	Ropner Shipping
1685	Olympic Banner	Oil tanker	24 November 1972	128,561	Carlow Maritime Panama

No.	Name	Type	Date Completed	Tonnage	Owner
1686	Olympic Brilliance	Oil tanker	7 September 1973	128,561	Lakeport Navigation Co.
1687	Cancelled				
1688	Iron Somersby	Bulk carrier	7 December 1971	57,250	Ropner Shipping
1689	Barbro	Bulk carrier	18 February 1972	61,955	Mascot A/S
1690	Belinda	Bulk carrier	30 June 1972	61,955	Mascot A/S
1691	Mount Newman	Bulk carrier	16 November 1973	65,131	Furness Withy
1692	Canadian Bridge	Bulk carrier	29 November 1974	65,135	Bibby Shipping
1693	World Cavalier	Oil tanker	12 June 1974	138,025	Worldwide Shipping Co.
1694	Lotorium	Oil tanker	27 February 1975	138,037	Shell Tankers Ltd
1695	Lampas	Oil tanker	17 November 1975	161,632	Shell Tankers Ltd
1696	Lepeta	Oil tanker	26 July 1976	161,632	Shell Tankers Ltd
1697	Leonia	Oil tanker	30 December 1976	161,626	Shell Tankers Ltd
1698	Lima	Oil tanker	3 June 1977	161,632	Shell Tankers Ltd
1699	Essi Camilla	Bulk carrier	5 January 1976	63,509	Ruud Pedersen A/S
1700	Cancelled				
1701	Lackenby	Bulk carrier	5 July 1977	64,640	Ropner Shipping
1702	Cancelled				
1703	Cancelled				
1704	Coastal Corpus Christi	Oil tanker	25 March 1980	172,147	Woodstock Shipping Co.
1705	Coastal Hercules	Oil tanker	25 March 1980	172,147	Pomona Shipping Co.
1706	Cancelled				
1707	Cancelled				
1708	Appleby	Bulk carrier	31 October 1978	64,641	Ropner Shipping
1709	Hornby Grange	Products tanker	20 June 1979	39,626	Furness Withy & Co.
1710	Elstree Grange	Products tanker	24 October 1979	39,626	Furness Withy & Co.
1711	Isomeria	LPG carrier	30 April 1982	42,069	Shell Tankers Ltd
1712	Isocardia	LPG carrier	29 October 1982	42,069	Shell Tankers Ltd
1713	Galloway Princess	Ferry	22 April 1980	6,268	British Rail (Sealink)
1714	Ravenscraig	Bulk carrier	14 December 1979	64,651	British Steel Corporation
1715	St Anselm	Ferry	16 October 1980	7,003	British Rail (Sealink)
1716	St Christopher	Ferry	6 March 1981	6,996	British Rail (Sealink)
1717	St David	Ferry	24 July 1981	7,109	British Rail (Sealink)

No.	Name	Type	Date Completed	Tonnage	Owner
1718	British Skill	Oil tanker	26 April 1983	66,034	British Petroleum Ltd
1719	British Success	Oil tanker	14 February 1984	66,034	British Petroleum Ltd
1720	British Steel	Bulk carrier	19 October 1984	90,831	British Steel Corporation
1721	English Star	Refrigerated cargo ship	7 January 1986	10,291	Blue Star Line
1722	Scottish Star	Refrigerated cargo ship	2 April 1985	10,291	Blue Star Line
1723	Auckland Star	Refrigerated cargo ship	21 January 1986	10,291	Blue Star Line
1724	Canterbury Star	Refrigerated cargo ship	1 July 1986	10,291	Blue Star Line
1725	Ironbridge	Bulk carrier	23 September 1987	90,707	British Steel Corporation
1726	Schiehallion	SWOPS vessel	31 December 1997	85,003	British Petroleum Ltd
1727	Fort Victoria	Fleet replenishment ship	4 May 1990	31,565	Admiralty
1728	Knock Allen	Oil tanker	22 April 1992	79,902	Fred Olsen & Co.
1729	Cancelled				

The only time the four Sealink sister ships were ever together in the same port: *Galloway Princess*, *St Christopher*, *St Anselm* and *St David*.

No.	Name	Type	Date Completed	Tonnage	Owner
1730	Cancelled				
1731	Knock Clune	Oil tanker	7 July 1993	86,266	Fred Olsen & Co.
1732	Knock Dun	Oil tanker	23 October 1994	78,843	Fred Olsen & Co.
1733	Cancelled				
1734	Lowlands Trassey	Bulk carrier	12 May 1995	83,830	Trassey Shipping (Fred Olsen)
1735	Knock An	Oil tanker	8 August 1996	79,244	Fred Olsen & Co.
1736	Knock Muir	Oil tanker	2 February 1996	79,001	Fred Olsen & Co.
1737	Cancelled				
1738	Cancelled				
1739	Glomar C.R. Luigs	Drill ship	1 July 2000	47,079	Global Marine Ltd
1740	Glomar Jack Ryan	Drill ship	1 July 2000	47,079	Global Marine Ltd
1741	Hartland Point	Ferry	11 December 2002	23,235	Andrew Weir
1742	Anvil Point	Ferry	17 January 2003	23,235	Andrew Weir

Note: Yard number 694 is omitted because it was allocated in error to a fixed pontoon and *not* a vessel.

Job No. 5139 Sea Quest Oil Rig, completed on 5 July 1966 with a gross tonnage of 7,900 for BP Clyde Tanker Company. Sea Quest was the first rig to discover the oil reserves in the North Sea.

Job No. 5320 The construction of Falkland Flexi port, a floating harbour complex for the Falkland Islands to replace the damaged harbour facilities after the Argentine invasion. It was completed in February 1984.

Job No. 5500 The conversion of container vessel *Contender Bezant* into RFA Argus Helicopter Training Ship for the UK Admiralty. It was completed on 1 June 1988.

Abbreviations

Alfred Holt	Ocean Steamship Company (Blue Funnel Line)
Andrew Weir	Andrew Weir & Company (Bank Line)
OSNC	Oceanic Steam Navigation Company
P&O	Peninsular & Oriental Steam Navigation Company
PSNC	Pacific Steam Navigation Company
Royal Mail	Royal Mail Lines Limited
Shaw Savill	Shaw Savill & Albion Company
Union Castle	Union Castle Mail Steamship Company

Index